Here are some of the fascinating people you'll meet in *Where There's a Will . . .*

The Joker who left more than half a million dollars to the mother who gave birth to the greatest number of children in the ten years after his death.

The Wit (German poet Heinrich Heine) who stipulated that in order to inherit, his wife must remarry: 'Then,' he said in his will, 'there will be at least one man to regret my death.'

The Bard. Why did Shakespeare leave his wife his 'second-best bed'?

The Frustrated Actor who left his head to be used as the skull of Yorick in a production of *Hamlet*.

The Movie Star who left enough for booze and cocktail snacks 'because I don't want my friends to go away sober or serious.'

The Bawdyhouse Madame who left an embarrassing bequest to the town reformer who swore he would put her out of business.

The Lawyer who willed 100,000 francs to the local madhouse: I obtained this money out of those who pass their lives in litigation; in bequesting it for the use of lunatics I only make restitution.'

WHERE THERE'S A WILL

ROBERT S. MENCHIN

CORGI BOOKS

A DIVISION OF TRANSWORLD PUBLISHERS LTD

WHERE THERE'S A WILL
A CORGI BOOK 0 552 11861 3

Originally published in Great Britain
by Frederick Muller Ltd.

PRINTING HISTORY
Frederick Muller edition published 1980
Corgi edition published 1981

This book is set in 10 pt. Times Roman

Corgi Books are published by Transworld Publishers Ltd.,
Century House, 61–63 Uxbridge Road,
Ealing, London, W5 5SA

Made and printed in the United States of America by
Offset Paperbacks, Dallas, Pennsylvania

For Marylin,
Jonathan and Scott

CONTENTS

"I must say, before I begin, that the deceased had a most delicious sense of humor."

Foreword

The sad and humorous episodes which make up this volume defy an ordinary approach to will-making. Simplification in wills is quite impossible, because no one, no matter what he may think, is a simple person. Life is complicated. That is one of its pleasures. Those who look for simple formulas or wider generalization end up in trouble, for each testator is a separate and unique gathering of cells.

The last caprice of each and every human being represents a monopoly, since most of us express ridicule for all caprices except our own. But this book may be a "How to Do It" insofar as it may evoke admiration for the kind of bravery that allows the suppressions of a lifetime to be defiantly proclaimed in a will. After all, says the testator, who can hurt me in the grave?

Jurisprudence may be able to standardize warehouse receipts or check forms, but wills continue to reflect the diversity of man's personality. As a lover of variety and individuality, I suggest we are fortunate to have in this book of fascinating and entertaining stories: the man who took God in as a business partner; the many people who defy death in their own special way by writing their will in verse or treating their will as a practical joke; not to mention the young man who literally swallowed an objectionable will. My own personal favorite is the man who would disown his natural son if he grew a mustache.

Caprice? Perhaps. But where there are a few last caprices

you can be sure the culture is less than free, the income is meager, ambition for better standards of living has not yet been born, and the people are without aspirations, frustrations or ulcers. In many societies today—in parts of Africa and India, for example—possessions can be put into a small ditty bag, and the complicated problems of disposing of one's worldly goods do not arise. Wills are for the sophisticates of our planet.

For nearly half a century as a member of the bar, I have advised a good number of these "sophisticates" and helped them draw wills. We usually begin by reviewing their lists of beneficiaries, and I marvel at the wild conglomeration of conflicting desires and the compromises between love and hate that such a list represents.

In a lawyer's office, Will Time is an occasion for unmasking and for all kinds of spiritual undressing. As each client concedes his mortality and faces up to the problems of disposition, the lawyer's desk becomes the psychologist's couch. Face to face, many of the wealthy who have hated the government give instructions which make bequests to the state and Federal treasuries—in the form of inheritance taxes—rather than leave the money to a pet charity or cause. Then there is the dominant male, often a delightful and casual philanderer, who expresses a desire to have his dead hand control the love life of his surviving wife. She is to receive substantial income until the day of her remarriage. Thus does the testator induce his widow to live in so-called "sin" with a lush income from the estate rather than get married to an impecunious male and have her income cut off.

However, in our society wives may not be totally disowned; even husbands often may not be cut off without a sou. This so-called "dower" is the sovereign state's answer to the testator, preventing the too great expression of hate that would leave the surviving spouse without that guessed-at compromise between duty and affection—often, one-third of the will-maker's estate.

At Will Time, parents are confronted with the fact that all offspring are not equally loved. Then begins the attempt to balance the books—emotional as well as financial.

In this collection of odd and curious wills, the foolish and the wise share a common defiance of the inevitable. While their presence in this book strongly suggests that they are no longer with us, it is a lively and colorful cast of characters that Bob Menchin offers. It is ironic that many relatively unknown and unsung testators may, through this book, be more frequently quoted in death than they ever were in life.

—*Morris L. Ernst*

Nantucket, Mass.

A rich American wrote a will leaving every dollar he possessed to a girl he used to watch in the theatre. He did not know her and the only reason he made the bequest was that her turned up nose amused him.

"A will," writes Bulwer, "is wealth's last caprice."

The Last Caprice

In 1720, an Englishman named Edmund Curll published a curious and now very rare book containing the wills of celebrated personalities of his time. Curll was a forerunner of today's gossip columnist. He would spice his books with biographical sketches, anecdotes and intimate facts about the lives of the will makers—all designed to fan the imagination of his public and brighten conversation at the local pub. A prominent statesman of his day described Curll as "one of the new terrors of death."

Obviously, he was not without readers.

Wills have a special appeal to those contemplating the mysteries of human nature. Perhaps more than any other human document they reflect the character of the writer and reveal his relationship to family, friends and the world at large. Man's nature, his prejudice, his interests, his eccentricities and the full range of his virtues and vices, can be found in the pages of wills.

An eighteenth century writer on the subject wrote, "So surely as a berry indicates the soundness of the root, the flower of the bulb, so does a man's last will tell of the goodness or foulness of the heart which conceived it."

A man's last words deserve our attention. When that man happens to be one of history's immortals, the interest is heightened. When, for example, William Shakespeare says in his will that he leaves his wife his *"second best bed,"* he is inviting the raised eyebrow and whispered innuendo for ages to come.

When Benjamin Franklin bequeathed to his son William certain land holdings in Nova Scotia explaining, *"The part he acted against me in the late war, which is of public notoriety, will account for my leaving him no more of an estate he endeavored to deprive me of . . ."* we sense the deep hurt that Franklin felt and we begin to understand the chasm that developed between father and son.

Is there anything written by Rabelais, the fifteenth century satirist, that is as quickly revealing as his one sentence last will and testament?—*"I have nothing, I owe a great deal; the rest I give to the poor."*

If these choice morsels from the past lead you to conclude that will-writing is a dying art, you have made a weak pun but an accurate observation. Wills just aren't what they used to be. When Edmund Curll's presses worked far into the night to meet the demands of a clamoring public, wills made provocative reading; today such wills are rare.

Most wills today are formal legal documents and only a relative or close friend would find it of interest. A will is, by definition, a written instrument for the disposition of property after death. Most will writers keep close to the business at hand. Resigned to the fact that they cannot take it with them, they approach the problem of giving it away with precision, solemnity and understandable ill-humor. This conventional approach simplifies matters for the lawyers, the judges and the heirs but for the rest of us, it takes all the fun out of minding other people's business. The legalistic format and the recitation of contents—give or take a few thousand or a few million—makes most wills hopelessly dull reading. The fact that they enrich someone other than ourself makes them downright annoying.

Happily, there are those cherished few who break from convention and use their wills to strike a highly individualistic note. When that happens, as in the case of John B. Kelly,

22

the results can be something special—a collector's delight. The Kelly document stands as eloquent proof that a will need not be dull; that a will can be warm, personal and witty without defeating its purposes or endangering its legal status.

Perhaps others, inspired by this classic will and encouraged by the great interest it has evoked, will take advantage of a similar opportunity available to them. But do not take Kelly's *"I will attempt to write my own will"* literally or be misled by the informal language and casual tone. Kelly drew his will with the cooperation and advice of his attorney—as should you.

That's as far as we go on this point. Other books, and there are many, explain why it is important that you have a will, discuss the legal consideration as they differ in each of the fifty states and issue proper warning against preparing a will without the benefit of legal advice. "Where There's A Will" has a more frivolous purpose.

This book contains some odd and curious specimens rescued from the pigeon-holes of obscurity. While I cherish each of the bits and pieces that went into the mosaic that follows, I have a sense of deep frustration about the missing wills, the unknown and unheralded fragments that leave the picture incomplete. They lie somewhere, gathering dust and slowly disintegrating, surrounded by millions of other wills, embedded in billions of words, and the task of sifting the worthy ones from the unworthy is somewhat akin to isolating a few grams of gold from thousands of tons of rock.

This book is an expanded, enlarged and updated version of "The Last Caprice," which was published in 1963. Besides providing material included in the book, "The Last Caprice," with its wide distribution in the U.S. and abroad, helped to generate some of the material which appears here. Once you let people know of your interest in this delightfully off-beat subject a windfall is liable to come your way at any time. ("I've got a good one for you . . . did you know that Washington's dentist left a will leaving his nephew a tooth that he personally extracted from the great man's mouth . . .").

I have tried to make "Where There's A Will," a book that both layman and professional can enjoy. If there is any truth to the saying that half the world delights in slander and the other half in believing it, then both the author and the reader will reap their just rewards for there are plenty of gossipy tidbits in old wills. Those who can take their gossip or leave it will find entertainment perhaps more suited to their taste. Students of jurisprudence will find wills with enough legal jargon and subtle points of law to brighten the day of any Philadelphia lawyer. Searchers of literary merit will find many beautifully written passages and will-turned phrases —sometimes in the most surprising places. Those with an historical bent will gain a new perspective of men and events of the past and collectors of the bizarre and the curious can approach the subject of wills expecting much. They will not be disappointed.

Robert S. Menchin

Unlikely Heirs

That so few now dare to be eccentric marks the chief danger of our time.

JOHN STUART MILL

Conrad Cantzen was a familiar figure along Broadway. A gentleman-pauper and actor of bit parts, he panhandled for meals, discreetly snatched food where he could, wore fingerless gloves and a filched boutonnière. When he died in 1945 at the age of seventy-eight, the Actor's Fund paid his hospital bill and buried him in its plot in Kensico Cemetery.

A will was discovered in his dismal, solitary room a few days after he was buried. It began:

I leave the Conrad Cantzen Shoe Fund for the people who can't buy shoes, even if they are not paid-up members of Equity. Many times I have been on my uppers, and the thinner the soles of my shoes were, the less courage I had to face the managers in looking for a job.

Along with the will went the sum of $226,608.34, a hundred thousand dollars of it in savings banks, the rest in government and gilt-edge bonds. Altogether almost a quarter of a million dollars.

Today any professional actor, temporarily at liberty and

making the rounds in a pair of run-down shoes, can "do the shoe bit"—a commonplace experience in Broadway circles. Doing the shoe bit starts with a visit to Actors Equity, at 226 West Forty-seventh Street, and culminates with a visit to the Thom McAn Shoe Store at 129 West Forty-second Street, New York. Compliments of Conrad Cantzen, Actor.

★

Jack Luke of Rotheringham, England, who died in 1812, left a penny to every child who attended his funeral (over seven hundred youngsters were there). All the poor women in the parish were left one shilling each and the bell ringers were left half a guinea each, to *strike off one peal of grand bobs* at the exact moment of his burial.

Mr. Luke's final bequest was for forty dozen penny loaves which were to be thrown down from a parish church steeple at noon on every Christmas Day forever.

★

Mrs. Sylvia Ann Howland Wilks died in 1951 leaving $100 million and a will bequeathing the money to sixty-three charitable institutions . . . and to ten distant relatives spread throughout the country. Mrs. Wilks hired a genealogist to locate these relatives, the descendants of Gideon Howland, a great grandfather who started the family fortune in the whaling business in New Bedford, Connecticut. Although she made considerable effort to locate her distant relatives in order to include them in her will, she made no effort to contact them during her lifetime.

Mrs. Wilks inherited her millions from her mother, the infamous Hetty Green. Considered among the richest women in the world and often referred to as "the wizard of Wall Street," Hetty Green was known as much for her miserliness and eccentricities as she was for her wealth. Her mother's irrational attitude toward money carried over to Sylvia. The ten surprised inheritors of Sylvia Wilks' wealth were so elderly that the bequest had little meaning.

★

Bread bequests were once popular as Christmas legacies in England. In the year 1660 a pastor named Arthur Colfe left in trust money to buy 104 sweet penny loaves for the neediest in East London's slum district of Deptford. Three hundred years of interest has swelled the fund to the point where today, instead of a penny loaf, the beneficiary is entitled to a two-shilling (twenty-eight-cent) voucher for the purchase of food.

★

One charity bequest calls for the baking of a huge plum pudding, to weigh in excess of three hundred pounds, for needy families in the Devonshire town of Paignton. This bequest, however, comes only once in fifty years. The last plum pudding was distributed in 1951; the next is due in 2001.

★

The privacy that Howard Hughes sought during his life eluded him even after death. The wasted, 92-pound eccentric, suffering from medical neglect and drug addiction, died on an emergency flight from Acapulco to a Houston hospital. His death let loose a stream of bizarre disclosures, each bringing greater notoriety to the tortured genius who was considered America's richest man. Hughes' highly diversified and far-flung empire was valued at $2.3 *billion* in the late sixties and was probably worth a great deal more at the time of his death in 1976.

The Hughes fortune included giant corporations, major defense contractors Hughes Aircraft and Hughes Helicopter, Las Vegas hotels and casinos, a TV station, a TV network, large land holdings in California, Nevada, Texas and Louisiana and miscellaneous properties that would require a book by itself to list. Even a small portion of the mind-boggling Hughes wealth would make a man very rich and it was inevitable that many would try for it.

How and when the Hughes estate is distributed will depend on the verification of a valid will—if there is a valid will. A Hughes aid has testified that Hughes once mentioned that he had drawn up a handwritten will. When the aide asked where it was, the wasted, drug-addicted and isolated billionaire snapped back, "You don't think I'm going to tell you where it is, do you?"

Over 40 wills surfaced immediately after the death of the strange billionaire, each claiming to be the last will and testament of Howard Hughes. Hughes's peculiar habits and obsessive secrecy created the kind of confusion that makes it difficult to distinguish the real from the fake. The search for an authentic Hughes will led to some strange developments. Among the 40-odd wills that emerged to claim a portion of the Hughes estate, the most famous was the "Mormon Will," which takes its name from the fact that it was found on an official's desk in the headquarters of the Church of Jesus Christ of Latter-day Saints in Salt Lake City. The "Mormon Will" stipulated that one-sixteenth of Hughes' money was to go to Melvin Dummar, a Utah gas-station operator. Dummar maintained that he once picked up a disheveled old man, on a lonely Nevada roadside, and gave him a lift to Las Vegas. The man he gave a lift to turned out to be Howard Hughes. The gesture won a place in Hughes's heart and, even more important, a place in his will. Noah Dietrich, Hughes' estranged right hand man believed that the "Mormon Will" was authentic. After a seven month trial, in which handwriting experts debated the authenticity of the three-page document, a Nevada jury concluded that the will was a fake and Dummar was left with no legitimate claim on the Hughes estate.

In another attempt to locate a genuine will, the wife of a Hughes executive enlisted the services of a Dutch-born Hollywood psychic. Using a pair of Hughes shoes to activate his extrasensory perceptions, the psychic reported that he had a vision of a will reposing "in a bank in Houston, an old bank, partly fallen down or rebuilt." He could pinpoint the bank, he said, if he had photographs of all the banks in Houston to stimulate his psychic vision. Immediately agents were dispatched to Houston where they carefully photographed every bank in the city. The result was a beautiful set of bank snapshots but the search proved to be just one more wild goose chase.

Now the struggle for control of Hughes Aircraft Company, the biggest prize in the package, centers on three men —William Lumis, a 49-year-old Texas-born cousin of Hughes who saw him only twice in his life, the last time when Lumis was nine. The others in the three cornered power play are two Hughes executives who had long experience managing his business interests, though they saw him only once in his last twenty years. They are playing for high stakes. Hughes Aircraft, an aerospace manufacturer, is one of the nation's major defense contractors. The company employs 40,000 people—one third of them engineers and scientists—in more than a dozen U.S. cities and in thirteen countries. Years ago Air Force Secretary Harold Talbott went so far as to say that the malfunctioning of Hughes Aircraft Co. could imperil the nation. The struggle for control of Hughes Aircraft is such that barring a settlement, the U.S. Supreme Court may be called upon to resolve the matter.

All of this could have been avoided had Hughes left a will. But even while interested parties continue the search, there is little hope that a signed testament will ever be uncovered. Many of the people who knew him best, aware of his tendency to put things off and to remain aloof from personal attachments, believe that he deliberately avoided writing a will. One of his aids, Gordon Margulis, has expressed the opinion that Hughes, when he faced up to death simply said, "Screw them all."

★

From the will of a Philadelphia industrialist who died in 1947 . . .

"To my wife I leave her lover, and the knowledge that I wasn't the fool she thought I was.

"To my son I leave the pleasure of earning a living. For twenty-five years he thought the pleasure was mine. He was mistaken.

"To my daughter I leave $100,000. She will need it. The only piece of business her husband ever did was to marry her.

"To my valet I leave the clothes he has been stealing from me for ten years. Also the fur coat he wore last winter while I was in Palm Beach.

"To my chauffeur, I leave my cars. He almost ruined them and I want him to have the satisfaction of finishing the job.

"To my partner, I leave the suggestion that he take some clever man in with him at once if he expects to do any business."

A Dying Art

More people have died because they have made
their wills than because they were sick.
SPANISH PROVERB

In the nineteenth century a man named McAllister, residing in southern Scotland, left each of his daughters her weight in one-pound bank notes. By this provision, one daughter, being considerably stouter than the other, received the equivalent of thirty thousand dollars more than her sister.

★

As an artist's model in Paris during the early part of the nineteenth century, Charles-Alis Dubosc spent hour after hour in fixed immobility, his whole body frozen in position. From his vantage point on the platform he could observe the frustrations, disappointments and struggle with poverty of the young painters and sculptors who managed to scrape up the few francs for model's fees. Perhaps he could help.

Subsisting on scraps, dressed in rags, Dubosc saved nearly all he earned not even allowing himself the luxury of living on his meagre income. When he died there was 200,000 francs with which to realize the plan which is contained in this moving document, his last will and testament.

"I, the undersigned Charles-Alis Dubosc, declare this to be my last will and testament. Having begun my life as an artist's model in 1834 at the age of seven, and having continued to serve as a model till I was sixty-three, I have necessarily passed my life among the most distinguished artists; I wish, therefore, that at my decease the little fortune I have earned and have left behind me should be useful to artists—it is from them I have drawn all I possess.

"Consequently, I constitute as my universal heir the Institut de France, Academie des Beaux-Arts, that it may dispose of my succession in the manner following: After the payment of all duties and rights, the capital shall be invested in the Three per Cent. rentes, and the arrears of such rentes shall once in each year be distributed in equal portions to such young painters and sculptors as shall have been elected competitors for the Prix de Rome, such sums to be remitted to them at the time they are admitted to the enclosed quarters in which they work.

"Made and written by my own hand at Paris this 22d day of July, 1850. Signed. Dubosc."

★

While some Americans employ elaborate tax shelters and trust devices to keep Uncle Sam from getting any of their money during their lifetime or after, others make a special effort to give Uncle Sam all or part of their estate by putting the U.S. government into their will.

Money willed to the United States is recorded on a special account on the Treasury's books labelled "Gifts to the United States." As of 1978, the U.S. government had inherited $45,802,912.31 from generous patriotic citizens.

These gifts go into the government's checking account and can be spent in any way that the government sees fit. You can, however, bequeath money to special funds authorized by Congress—certain Department of Health, Education and Welfare activities or the Library of Congress, for example —by indicating this desire in your will.

*"Jameson, you scoundrel, you've been
editing my will again!"*

Courtesy Burr Shafer

★

William Berns, a wealthy Madison Avenue jeweler, died on April 20, 1962. According to the terms of his will, his estate, valued at $250,000, goes to the United States Treasury *for general governmental purposes.* The will reads:

I make this bequest in appreciation of the freedom and liberty afforded in this country to all citizens, irrespective of race, creed or color.

Berns wrote these words on January 24, 1961, four days after President Kennedy, in his inauguration address, said to the American people, "Ask not what your country can do for you—ask what you can do for your country."

★

In a will made in 1434, a member of the Norton family of Southwick, London, left all he had *"to be used unto the end of the world for the benefit of the poor, the hungry, the thirsty, the naked, the sick, and the wounded, and prisoners,"* and he appointed the Houses of Parliament as his executors.

The will was set aside on the ground that the testator was insane and the estate was transferred to the natural heirs.

★

On December 6 and 7, 1922, a total of 203 persons entered the Oakland court of Judge E. S. Robinson to claim their share of a $350,000 bequest left by San Francisco nightclub-owner Joseph Bisagno. Among the heirs were society women, waitresses, matrons, bootblacks, headwaiters, actresses (Broadway star Marjorie Rambeau), waiters, hatcheck girls, judges, attorneys, physicians, businessmen, city officials, café owners, bartenders and saloonkeepers. All, said Mr. Bisagno in his will, *"friends who have been kind to me."*

★

Unable to make up his mind about which of his three deserving nephews to make his heir, Henry Durrell decided to let fate decide the matter. In his will he stipulated that the choice should be made by a throw of the dice.

On March 15, 1921, three young men met at their late uncle's estate in Bermuda to carry out the terms of the will. A pair of dice was passed around and minutes later Richard Durrell emerged as the new owner of the palatial estate on the shore of Hamilton Harbor, the show place of Bermuda.

★

Under a century-old legacy provided for by a man named John Orr, interest on an approximately four-thousand-dollar fund is set aside annually for four Scotch brides. Checks to the equivalent of thirty dollars each are sent to the tallest, shortest, oldest and youngest bride married during the year at St. Cyprus, Scotland.

★

When prominent Canadian attorney Charles Millar died, friends asked his former law partner whether Millar left a will.

"I've found some writing in the form of a will," he replied, "but it's not a will—it's a joke. We're searching for the actual will now."

The "joke" turned out to be The Last Will and Testament of Charles Vance Millar and a few months later his former law partner was defending this "joke" in court—and defending it successfully for twelve years against repeated attacks from outraged citizens, disappointed relatives and righteous reformers who "didn't get the joke."

In the will, Millar explains it this way:

This will is necessarily uncommon and capricious because I have no dependents or near relations and no duty rests upon me to leave any property at my death and what I do leave is proof of my folly in gathering and retaining more than I required in my lifetime.

This preamble to Charles Millar's will suggests what follows: twelve clauses consisting mostly of good-natured pranks and a final caper that sent hundreds of Canadian women off on a raucous race with the stork that is now known as the celebrated "Baby Derby."

Among Millar's pranks:

To the Hon. W. E. Raney, A. M. Orpen and Reverend Samuel D. Chown, each one share in the Ontario Jockey Club providing three years from my death each of them becomes enrolled as shareholders in the share register of the Club. . . .

Dr. Chown and Judge Raney were dedicated foes of all forms of gambling, especially horse racing. Mr. Orpen operated a track in direct competition to the Jockey Club. On August 27, 1927, Dr. Chown and Judge Raney became members of the club, but five minutes later they sold their shares for fifteen hundred dollars each; Mr. Orpen retained his membership.

To each Protestant Minister exercising his clerical functions . . . and to each Orange Lodge in Toronto I give one share of the O'Keefe Brewery Company of Toronto, Limited.

Of the 260 eligible clergymen, 91 accepted their shares. Of the 114 Orange Lodges, 103 did likewise. Most of the beneficiaries under this clause sold their shares and turned the $58.20 they received for each share over to charity.

Clause number nine in the will turned over Millar's home in Jamaica to three acquaintances. These men each had an abiding dislike for one another, so naturally Millar thought it would be a good idea if they lived together for a while.

All this was by way of a curtain-raiser to the fertility farce inspired by the last bequest in Millar's will:

All the rest and residue of my property . . . at the expiration of ten years from my death . . . to the Mother who has . . . given birth in Toronto to the greatest number of children.

Canada was unprepared for the hijinks that followed. Throughout his seventy-three years of life Charles Millar was a prim, painfully proper bachelor, hardly the type who would inspire Canadian ladies to fill the maternity wards to overflowing. But there it was: the courts upheld the bequest, the money was good and the race was on.

Toronto newspapers quickly dubbed the contest "The Stork Derby" and publicized the event with feature stories as the participants carved new notches on their cribs and new entries became all too apparent. As the mothers approached the finish line, box scores were published and Canadians with sporting blood placed wagers and cheered their favorites to greater heights of achievement.

Meanwhile, Millar's second cousins and even more remote relatives hired lawyers to litigate the will out of existence. Contesters of the will claimed that the clause "encouraged immorality" and was "against public policy" but Millar was as good an attorney as he was a prankster. The will was legally sound—again and again the court found in favor of "the unknown mother."

On May 30, 1938, Judge MacDonnell of Surrogate Court, Toronto, distributed the estate. With interest added it came to $568,106. Four prolific Toronto mothers, each with nine children born during the ten-year period, shared the prize in accordance with the terms of the will.

Mrs. Pauline Mae Clark claimed ten births during the period but her record was somewhat marred by the fact that only five children were also her husband's. To settle this sticky situation as well as the claim of Mrs. Lilie Kenny (four of her ten children were stillborn) consolation prizes of $12,500 were awarded to the runners-up.

In the summer of 1936, when she had her last baby, one of the winners, Mrs. Arthur Timleck, announced wearily that she was through: from here on she intended to practice—and preach—birth control. Charlie Millar would have gotten a chuckle out of that.

★

Discouraged by years of failure and defeat, Paul Duhalde, dealer in precious stones, opened his account book to a fresh page, entered the date—September 27, 1719—and wrote these words:

I have resolved to enter into a partnership with God, promising and undertaking to fulfill all the within-mentioned articles; and I enjoin my heirs, whoever they may be, to carry out these my intentions in case I should die before accomplishing them myself.

Shortly thereafter the tide of events changed. Duhalde married the daughter of a wealthy merchant and his business prospered as he gained new skill and confidence as a trader. Never failing to meet his obligations to his silent, invisible partner, Duhalde drew half the profits at regular intervals and distributed them to the poor "in the name of God."

Some ten years after the partnership began, the diamond merchant was struck down with a serious illness. In a hastily prepared will, written in the third person, he said:

"Back to reading of the will in just a minute,
friends, but first, a word about our law firm,
Linder, Hall, Smoot and Carver."

In the books which contain the minutes of his affairs there are several articles touching matters that concern the poor; he begs his executor to examine these articles with the greatest accuracy, and to see that they are carried out with the strictest attention.

When Duhalde died two months after making his will, his executors found many packets of precious gems marked "Half for the poor" at the merchant's shop. In his final days Duhalde had expressed the desire that his partner's share, the half for the poor, be given to the Hospital General and so the administrators of that institution claimed the bequest.

Duhalde's young widow balked at the idea of sharing the legacy and the dispute had to be resolved in court. Speaking for the widow, the guardian asked that the will be set aside on the ground that the testator was not mentally competent to draw a will since "no sane man ever entered into partnership with God."

On April 3, 1726, Avocat-General D'Agnesseau handed down the decision that "the will shall be fulfilled according to the desire of the testator," and directed the widow to hand over to the hospital administrators the jewels constituting the legacy made by the testator—thereby closing the dramatic story of Paul Duhalde, dealer in diamonds, and his singular partnership with God.

★

The Prince of Darkness had his day in court. A wealthy Finnish landowner left a will bequeathing all of his vast property to the Devil. The will was set aside by the court, the Devil's claim disregarded and the property passed on to the legal heirs.

An old French proverb has it, "The Devil comes to us on wings but goes away limping."

★

In February 1963 Mrs. Geraldine Swift, an estate tax commissioner for the State of Arizona was going through the safe deposit box of James Kidd, a copper prospector who took off from his rented boarding house room one morning in 1949 and was never heard from again. A state law stipulates that property unclaimed after seven years should revert to the State of Arizona and Mrs. Swift opened Mr. Kidd's box to make an inventory of its contents. It showed that the miner owned thousands of shares of stock accumulated slowly during the twenties and thirties—his estate was worth $175,000. Tucked away in an envelope with rolled up brokers' receipts was a scrawled message written on a single page of ruled notebook paper . . .

Phoenix, Arizona, Jan. 2, 1946, this is my first and only will . . . I have no heirs and have not been married in my life, after all my funeral expenses have been paid and one hundred dollars to some preacher of the hospital to say farewell at my grave, sell all my property which is all in cash and stocks with E. F. Hutton & Co., Phoenix and have this balance money to . . .

—and now Mrs. Swift started in disbelief—

. . . . to go in a research or some scientific proof of a soul of the human body which leaves a death I think in time their can be a Photograph of soul leaving the human at death, James Kidd.

Superior Court Probate Judge Robert L. Myers ruled that the will was legitimate and said, "It is the job of the probate judge to carry out the wishes of a testator . . . If anyone can fulfill James Kidd's stipulations my job is to see that it is done."

Seventeen organizations and seventy-eight individuals put

up the $15 filing fee and were prepared to prove their skill at soul searching.

Among them was Nora Higgins, a housewife and self proclaimed clairvoyant who explained that the soul has no physical substance but consists of a hazy tinted form resembling that of the body, Jean Bright who claimed to be in constant contact "through my entire nervous system" with a dentist friend who died two years before, Dr. Richard Ireland who claimed the power to communicate with souls, and a lieutenant colonel in Thailand who flew in from Bangkok to fight his case based in part on his ability to describe the soul . . . "a most wonderful, delicate and small thing."

During the hearings Judge Myers received more than 4,500 letters of advice suggesting tests for proof of the soul's existence. When the hearing was over Judge Myers awarded the windfall—which had by that time grown to $250,000—to Barrow Neurological Institute in Phoenix. Barrow's officers won the money by testifying that they would use it to study the central nervous system. In 1971 the Arizona Supreme Court ruled that this was not the kind of soul-searching James Kidd had in mind. The court ruled to withhold the funds from Barrow and place them instead with one of four claimants that were more psychically oriented.

The bequest was finally awarded to the American Society for Psychical Research in New York City for "out of body" research to carry out the instructions of Kidd's strange will. The Society approached the problem of proving the existence of the soul by posing the question, "Is there some part of the human personality that is capable of operating outside the living body and continue to exist after the brain processes have ceased and the organism is decayed?" In other words, can the soul survive death? To find the answer a series of interviews was held to elicit the deathbed observations of 1,644 doctors and nurses in the United States who attended dying patients. For cross-cultural comparisons interviews were also held in India and 435 Indian reports of apparitions of dead relatives, visions of an afterlife and memories

46

reported by patients who had been revived from a near-death state were compared with U.S. cases.

The psychic scientists attempted to photograph the soul as Kidd had requested, using various types of cameras, film and video equipment, even a photomultiplier, a device more light sensitive than any camera. They failed.

According to Dr. Karlis Osis, the psychologist in charge of the study funded by Kidd's bequest, the results were, like most studies of that nature, inconclusive. However, Dr. Osis says that the money that James Kidd left behind in 1946 helped to discover thirty years later "increasing evidence that there is life after death and provide more information for a rational belief that something survives when the body dies. Careful analysis (of the interviews) confirmed our hypothesis of ecsomatic existence . . . not explained by purely medical, psychological and cultural factors."

An uneducated Arizona miner asked the questions and provided the initial funding for metaphysical research that may in some future generation solve the mystery of life after death . . .

★

In 1941 Ataullah K. Ozai-Durrani, an Afghan by birth, walked into the offices of the General Foods Corporation, set up a portable stove and cooked a batch of his rice in 60 seconds. His invention made him a very rich man when "Minute Rice" became a staple in American households coast to coast.

When the inventor died in 1964, he left half a million dollars to Harvard University specifically for the translation into English of the works of the poets Mirza Asadullah Khan Ghalib and Meer Taqui Meer, two obscure Persian poets.

New Yorker magazine's "Talk of the Town" applauded Ozai-Durrani's bequest for reasons other than its generosity to a literary cause . . .

". . . Consider, after all, the numbers of rich men (great, craggy-faced photography tycoons or transistor barons, who harangued on Individuality in their prime, and Enterprise, and made huge heaps of gold by the exercise of cunning, energy, brains, self-interest, force of personality, and so on) who on their deathbeds can think of nothing better to do with all the boodle than sending it along to the New Dormitory Fund of Renwick College or donate another gymnasium to St. Cuthbert's. This isn't to disparage these worthy causes, or any others, or to belittle their need for funds.

"But it's always seemed to us a pity that men with quantities of money to dispose of should dispose of it relentlessly in august and public-spirited bequests, as if the men themselves had never quite existed (except as bank accounts)—as if to use even a small part of one's money to express a prejudice, an occasional passion, something personal, would be degrading, and would bring laughter in the Great Beyond and public outcry from one's heirs.

"We take note here of the late Mr. Ozai-Durrani's handsome bequest, and feel the richer for it—richer by anticipation of the poems of two nineteenth-century Persian poets, even though (there is no telling) they may be terrible poets, but richer still because Mr. Ozai Durrani, inventor of 'Minute Rice,' was so keen about them, and let us glimpse it, and thus let us (now far away) glimpse him."

★

Everybody knew that Juan Potomachi was stagestruck. But no one realized just how stagestruck Senor Potomachi was until his death in 1955. In his will the Buenos Aires businessman left a part of his fortune to Teatro Dramatico —but on one condition. As he explains in his will:

All my life I wanted to be on the stage. Lack of talent prevented me at first from realizing that wish. Later my position in the community as a prominent businessman barred me altogether from the stage.
I leave 200,000 pesos ($50,000) to a fund from which talented young actors shall get yearly scholarships. My only

condition is that my head be preserved and used as a skull in Hamlet.

My dearest wish would be thereby fulfilled after all, as I would still have a part in a play after my death.

Odd as this conditional bequest is, it is not unique. John Reed, a gas lighter of the Walnut Street Theater of Philadelphia in the nineteenth century, never, as far as anyone knows, aspired to appear on the stage during his lifetime. He remained on the job for forty-four years, never absent, never late, never missing a performance. His death brought to light an ambition which, unless it was purely coincidental, inspired Senor Potomachi's bequest. A clause in John Reed's will reads as follows:

. . . my head to be separated from my body immediately after my death; the latter to be buried in a grave; the former, duly macerated and prepared, to be brought to the theater where I have served all my life, and to be employed to represent the skull of Yorick in the play Hamlet.

Comedians, it has been said, all want to play Hamlet. The dear departed all want to play Yorick.

★

During the search for an authentic Howard Hughes will, Sandra West told a friend, "You haven't seen anything yet until I am dead."

On March 10, 1977, the thirty-seven year old Mrs. West was found dead "of undetermined causes" in her luxurious Beverly Hills Mansion. The mysterious circumstances of her death caused hardly a stir in jaded, seen-everything Southern California. But when her will was found—a handwritten note scrawled in a wandering hand—they sat up and took notice.

Sandra Ilene West's will left the bulk of a three million dollar estate to her brother-in-law and directed that she be buried . . .

" . . . and thus, my ghoulish friends, ends the
first chapter of my last will and testament. Be
sure to listen again tomorrow . . . Will Grace
get her hooks on any of this money — she
who often called me an old goat? . . . Who are
the three characters, each destined to be cut
off with one lousy dollar? . . . And my faithful
wife, affectionately known as Old Howler —
will she find that the state law on widow's
rights, after all, could foil my clever lawyer and
good friend? . . ."

"next to my husband, in my lace nightgown . . . in my Ferrari, with the seat slanted comfortably."

King Tut's contemporaries would have understood. Ancient Egyptians buried their dead in a tomb along with food, drink and games with which to pass the time pleasantly in the next world. Mrs. West simply updated the ancient custom by substituting a few modern playthings. And Mrs. West wasn't kidding either. She stipulated that her brother-in-law's $2,500,000 bequest was to be cut down to $100,000 if he failed to follow her burial instructions to the letter.

When the will was presented for probate in the Superior Court of Los Angeles there was some doubt about whether it was possible to carry out the burial instructions. Mr. West, who had died nine years before, was buried with other members of his ranching and oil wealthy Texas family in a Masonic Cemetery in San Antonio. However, since there was no technical reason nor local ordinance that would prohibit burial in an automobile, Los Angeles Supreme Court Commissioner Franklin Dana said that the scrawled, handwritten will was bizarre but legal. He ordered the burial carried out according to Mrs. West's wishes.

On May 19, 1977, in the glare of Klieg lights and surrounded by reporters, television crews and hundreds of spectators, two truckloads of concrete were poured into a 9-foot long wooden crate containing the late Mrs. West, dressed in a lace nightgown, at the wheel of her baby-blue Ferrari "with the seat slanted comfortably." The concrete was needed to reinforce the sides of the large grave . . . and to discourage grave-robbing car thieves. As the crate was lifted by a crane and lowered into the grave some of the spectator's comments were overheard and reported in the next day's Los Angeles Times:

"They say you can't take it with you. But Mrs. West, she sure showed us you can take it with you."

"I sure hope she's got her driver's license with her, because she's got a long way to go."

- A policeman who helped hold back the crowd said, "I hope we don't have a wave of these burials now. Next thing you know, someone will want to be buried in a 747."

A spectator who knew the millionairess well said she would have enjoyed this, "but she would have wanted more hoopla." An old friend of Mrs. West said that she sought fame when she lived but that it had eluded her—until now.

★

So many wills are made each year with a dumb animal as the principal beneficiary that it can no longer be considered an eccentricity. Nowadays when a will naming a horse, dog, cat, monkey or parrot is admitted to probate, it does not even merit a three-line notice on page 56 of the *Times*.

However, no book on odd wills would be complete without at least one such entry. For the single, singular example, consider the will of Mr. Jonathan Jackson of Columbus, Ohio, who died early in the present century. Mr. Jackson left his money for the erection and maintenance of an elaborate home for cats, and in his will he gives careful, detailed specifications. The building is to contain dormitories, a refectory, areas for conversation, grounds for exercise, gently sloping roofs for climbing, an auditorium where the cat inmates may listen to accordian music, and "rat holes" for daily sport.

The testator gives as the reason for his bequest: *"It is man's duty as lord of animals to watch over and protect the lesser and feebler, even as God watches over and protects man."*

Why rats, supplied for the "sport" of his cherished cats, should not be entitled to similar protection, Mr. Jackson does not say.

★

Mr. Daniel Martinett, of Calcutta in the East Indies, was a simple man, a man who "lived profusely and died frugally":

First. In the most submissive manner I recommend my soul to Almighty God, &c.

Secondly. Now as to my worldly concerns, in the following manner: As to this fulsome carcase having already seen enough of worldly pomp, I desire nothing relative to it to be done, only its being stowed away in my old green chest, to avoid expense; for as I lived profusely, I die frugally.

Thirdly. The undertaker's fees come to nothing, as I won them from him at a game of billiards, in the presence of Mr. Thomas Morrice and William Perkes, at the said William Perkes' home, in February last.

Fourthly. To Henry Vansittart, Esq., Governor of Bengal, as an opulent man, I leave the discharge of all such sums of money that I shall stand indebted to indigent persons in the town of Calcutta.

Fifthly. To Mr. George Grey, Secretary of the Presidency, I bequeath all my sincerity.

Sixthly. To Mr. Simon Drose, Writer to the Secretary's office, all my modesty.

Seventhly. To Mr. Henry Higgenson, also of the Secretary's office, all the thoughts I hope I shall die possessed of.

Eighthly. To Thomas Forbes, all the worldly assurance which I had when I had taken a cheerful glass, though in fact a doleful cup.

As I have lived the make-game of a modern gentleman, being a butt for envy and a mark for malice, by acting a little out of the common road, though, thank God, never in a base way, I hope I may die in sincere love and charity to all men, forgiving all my persecutors, as I hope for forgiveness from my Creator.

As it lies not in my power to bequeath anything to my relations at home, I shall say nothing concerning them, as they have not for these six years past concerned themselves about me; excepting that I heartily wish them all well, and that my brothers and sisters may make a more prosperous voyage through this life than I have done.

(Signed) DANIEL MARTINETT

The original of this will was deposited in the Registry Office at Calcutta after the death of Daniel Martinett in 1825. The Governor accepted the legacy of debts referred to in item four—and paid them!

★

In a will published shortly after his death in 1950, George Bernard Shaw disposed of £367,233 ($1,028,252), a figure that makes the socialist author a capitalist of magnitude. *My Fair Lady,* the musical version of his play *Pygmalion,* had a seven-year run on Broadway and has been performed in Sweden, Mexico, Germany and Australia. The Shaw estate earned in excess of two million dollars on the Broadway production alone and the sales to the movies for an unprecedented five and a half million dollars swelled the estate beyond the realm of even Shaw's soaring imagination.

The author's detailed fourteen-page will begins with instructions for the cremation of the body. *"Personally,"* he writes in his will, *"I prefer the garden to the cloister."*

For many years before his death Shaw had been toying with the idea of leaving his estate for the purpose of creating and promoting a new phonetic alphabet which would simplify the spelling of English words and correct the disparity between the spoken word and the written word. Many of his friends felt that this was Shaw's way of dramatizing a cause he felt strongly about and that he would not really leave his money for so frivolous and futile a project. But Shaw meant what he said. Following a number of small personal bequests, the will directed that the residue of the estate should be used to determine how much time and effort could be saved by substituting a new forty-letter phonetic alphabet for the present English alphabet.

The British Museum and the Royal Academy of Dramatic Arts, confined in the use of the money by the specific directions, contested the will on the grounds that the alphabet trust was vague. In 1957, a compromise settlement was reached: only a limited portion of the estate would be used for the alphabet reform plan.

In a competition held shortly after to find a design for the new alphabet, 467 entries were received but not one was considered so outstanding as to merit its adoption as the Proposed British Alphabet. Four entries were chosen worthy of sharing the five-hundred-pound prize and the winners were asked to collaborate with scholars in the field in the hope that a final alphabet would evolve.

If, as, and when the alphabet is created, the real problem will be in gaining acceptance of the new phonetic alphabet by the English-speaking people of the world—a possibility that seems as remote as ever.

★

The Irish-born wife of playwright George Bernard Shaw left an estate of $263,200. In a long and verbose will (one sentence contained 151 words), Mrs. Shaw expressed the desire that her money be spent teaching her distinguished husband's compatriots *"self-control, elocution, deportment, the arts of personal contact and social intercourse."*

★

An eighteenth-century English gentleman apparently considered the Irish beyond reform. His will, probated in 1791, bequeaths the annual sum of ten pounds to be paid out by his estate for the following purpose:

It is my will and pleasure that this sum shall be spent in the purchase of a certain quantity of the liquor vulgarly called whiskey, and it shall be publicly given out that a certain number of persons, Irish only, not to exceed twenty, who may choose to assemble in the cemetery in which I shall be interred, on the anniversary of my death, shall have the same distributed to them. Further, it is my desire that each shall receive it by half-a-pint at a time till the whole is consumed, each being likewise provided with a stout oaken stick and a knife, and that they shall drink it all on the spot.

Knowing what I know of the Irish character, my conviction is, that with these materials given they will not fail to destroy each other, and when in the course of time the race comes to be exterminated, this neighborhood at least may, perhaps, be colonized by civilized and respected Englishmen.

★

A New York tailor who died in 1880 left these instructions in his will:

I own seventy-one pairs of trousers, and I strictly enjoin my executors to hold a public sale, at which these shall be sold to the highest bidder, and the proceeds distributed to the poor of the city.

I desire that these garments shall in no way be examined or meddled with, but be disposed of as they are found at the time of my death; and no purchaser to buy more than one pair.

The sale was actually held and the seventy-one pair of trousers were sold to seventy-one different purchasers. As each purchaser cut the thread to open the pockets, he found a packet containing a thousand dollars in bank notes—a reward, no doubt, for his good taste.

★

The president of the Colorado Woman's Christian Temperance Union received a bequest of five shares of brewery company stock *"as a marker for her family Bible."* The stock was willed to the temperance leader in 1934 by Charles F.

Hoechel, a Denver printer who was jailed at her insistence for printing liquor lists in violation of a Colorado liquor law.

To a Colorado banker, Mr. Hoechel left six hundred worthless shares in an oil company "which he sold to me on the damnedest misrepresentation and which he can use as a marker for *his* prayer book."

★

Ella Wendel, a picturesque New York recluse, died in 1931, leaving the bulk of a forty-million-dollar estate to charity. Altogether 2,303 separate claims—mostly by remote relatives—were filed against the will. So many challengers and their attorneys appeared to contest the will that they could not fit into the courtroom at one time.

Among the challengers was Thomas Patrick Morris, who mounted the witness stand and announced that he was the son of Miss Wendel's late brother, and therefore he had prior claim on the estate. Mr. Morris told a dramatic and minutely detailed story of his mother's secret marriage to the dead millionaire and offered in evidence a marriage certificate and a will which made him the sole heir to the Wendel fortune. For weeks the case was featured in front-page headlines and the legacy seemed to be within the reach of Mr. Morris, who confidently told reporters at a press conference that the money would be used "to help people who are poor and passed over by the world."

A small flaw stood between Mr. Morris and his philanthropic aspirations: the Bible in which the marriage certificate was inscribed was printed twenty-four years *after* the date on the certificate.

With that revelation, the case collapsed. The will turned out to be a clever forgery, and the forger a teller of tall tales. Of the 2,303 claimants to the Wendel estate, the court

*"What sort of will would you like to have,
Mr. Fignewton? . . . Short and simple? . . .
Or one that will go clear to the
Supreme Court?"*

Courtesy George Lichty,
and Field Enterprises, Inc.

recognized the rights of nine fifth-degree relatives. Among the losers was Thomas Patrick Morris, who was sentenced to three years in the state penitentiary for forging a will worth forty million dollars.

★

Vindictive Wills

*Thieves, as a last donation, leave advice to
their friends, physicians a nostrum, authors
a manuscript work, rakes a confession of their
faith in the virtue of the sex—all, the last
drivellings of their egotism and impertinence.
One might suppose that if anything could,
the approach and contemplation of death
might bring men to a sense of reason and
self-knowledge. On the contrary, it seems
only to deprive them of the little wit they
had, and to make them even more the sport
of their wilfulness and short-sightedness.*

WILLIAM HAZLITT,
"On Will-making"

From the Last Will and Testament of John Aylett, proved
in June 1781, pictorial retribution:

*I hereby direct my executors to lay out five guineas in
purchase of a picture of the viper biting the benevolent hand
of the person who saved him from perishing in the snow, if
the same can be bought for the money; and that they do, in
memory of me, present it to Edward Bearcroft, Esq., a*

King's Counsel, whereby he may have frequent opportunities for contemplating on it.

This I direct to be presented to him in lieu of a legacy of three thousand pounds which I had, by a former will, now revoked and burnt, left him.

★

Excerpts from the Last Will and Testament of Philip, Fifth Earl of Pembroke (seventeenth century):

Item: I give my body, for it is plain I cannot keep it; as you see, the chirurgeons are tearing it in pieces. Bury me, therefore; I hold lands and churches enough for that.

Item: I will have no monument, for then I must needs have an epitaph, and verses over my carcase: during my life I have had enough of these.

Item: I give all my wild beasts to the Earl of Salisbury, being very sure that he will preserve them, seeing that he refused the King a doe out of his park.

Item: I give nothing to my Lord Saye, and I do make him this legacy willingly, because I know that he will faithfully distribute it unto the poor.

Item: I bequeath to Thomas May, whose nose I did break at a mascarade, five shillings. My intention had been to give him more; but all who shall have seen his History of Parliament will consider that even this sum is too large.

Item: I give to the Lieutenant-General Cromwell one of my words, the which he must want, seeing that he hath never kept any of his own.

Item: I give up the ghost.

★

In his book *Country Lawyer*, Bellamy Partridge tells of the experience of his attorney father, Samuel Selden Partridge, in drawing a will for a client, Kate Vandenberg. ("Everybody in town knew what she was, though of course some of the men knew better than others.")

For years Kate was harassed by an ardent reformer who swore he would put her out of business. In fact, he ran for

*"Now read me the part again where I
disinherit everybody."*

village president on a platform that stressed ridding the town of vice in general—and Kate in particular. He never had the opportunity to make good on his promise, for shortly after he was elected, Kate died.

Kate left a will and in it she left a modest sum of money *"to one who had long been her valued friend"*—the village president!

★

Sometimes an incident offered up in Sunday supplements as authentic is really just the product of a writer's imagination. But no book on wills would be complete without this gem. Did it really happen? I've seen the incident described as a true story about a lady in Boise, Idaho and I've seen it dramatized in a hilarious episode in an Italian film. You decide:

A society matron placed an advertisement in the local newspaper offering to sell a brand new Cadillac in first class condition with low mileage for $50. Because nobody believed that it was a genuine offer it was some time before a buyer appeared. When one finally did he found that it was a real offer . . . and with no strings attached. It seems that the lady had just become a widow and her late husband specified in his will that his Cadillac or the proceeds from the sale of the car were to go to his girlfriend.

★

> *This fifth day of May,*
> *Being airy and gay,*
> *To trip not inclined,*
> *But of vigorous mind,*
> *And my body in health,*
> *I'll dispose of my wealth;*
> *And of all I'm to leave*
> *On this side the grave,*
> *To some one or other,*

I think to my brother.

But because I presaw
That my brothers-in-law
I did not take care,
Would come in for a share,
Which I noways intended,
Till their manners were mended—
And of that there's no sign.

I do therefore enjoin,
And strictly command,
As witness my hand,
That nought I have got
Be brought to hotch-pot.

And I give and devise,
Much as in me lies,
To the son of my mother,
My own dear brother,
To have and to hold
All my silver and gold,
As th' affectionate pledges
Of his brother,

John Hedges

This will in verse was proved in an English court in the year 1737.

★

Lord Redesdale, a lifetime foe of Communism, died in 1958 during his eightieth year of life. He left an estate of $361,000 to be shared by all but one of his daughters. The exception was Jessica, who had named her child Lenin.

Adolph J. Heimbeck, who died on July 10, 1958, wrote in his will:

1.

2.

3.

4.

DAVID
SNYDON

I leave nothing to my two sisters Hazel and Katherine as they revere Franklin D. Roosevelt and the taxes caused by him more than equalled their share.

★

Paul Revere left his money to his daughters and grandchildren except: *"It is my will that my grandson Frank (who now writes his name Francis Lincoln) eldest son of my late daughter Deborah, shall have no part of my estate, except one dollar which is here bequeathed to him."*

One can almost hear the sneer inside the parenthesis.

★

Ida Capers' life was a lonely one—except for her two Irish Setters, Brickland and Sunny Burch. She called them her "girls", sent out their pictures at Christmas, just as proud parents send snapshots of children and she wore two jewelled pins shaped like Irish Setters. Her dogs were her life, but Miss Capers worried constantly about what might happen to them when she was gone—who could possibly love them as she had?

Determined that her dogs should not suffer, Miss Capers wrote a will leaving the bulk of her estate to the Humane Society of Western Pennsylvania . . . and stipulating that Brickland and Sunny Burch be put to death.

When she died in Pittsburgh at the age of 72 and the story of Miss Capers' "death sentence" will became public, an avalanche of letters, telephone calls and wires poured in from dog lovers throughout the world. Small children and aging widows descended on the press and state officials pleading for clemency for Brickland and Sunny Burch. A Pennsylvania legislator said he would introduce a bill making it forever illegal for a will to order death for "any living creature, whether it be dogs or goldfish." The United Irish Society of Pittsburgh found a lawyer willing to defend the dogs—for free. A New York Stripteaser who owned 50 dogs threatened to undress on the courthouse steps to call attention to the setters' death sentence.

William Scranton, Governor of Pennsylvania at the time, spotted the story and interrupted a series of legislative meetings to inquire, "Can't we do something about this?" Within hours after the Governor's query, a special assistant attorney general went into Allegheny County Orphans Court, which handles the probate and interpretation of wills, and served notice that the Commonwealth of Pennsylvania wanted to be heard before the dogs died. But even before that, the Judge had already made up his mind. Brickland and Sunny Burch would not die until Ida Capers' estate was audited and that might take up to 15 months, maybe longer.

The dogs were never executed. A file in the Governor's office marked, "Dogs Saved From Death", is flowing over with messages offering warm and loving care to Brickland and Sunny Burch. Miss Capers rests in peace.

★

The Last Will and Testament of Herman Oberweiss, offered for probate in Texas, in June of 1934.

I am writing of my will mineself that des lawyir want he should have to much money he ask to many answers about the family. First think i dont want my brother Oscar to get a god dam thing i got he is a mumser and he done me out of four dollars fourteen years since.

I want it that Hilda my sister she gets the north sixtie akers of at where i am homing at now i bet she dont get that loafer husband of hers to brake twenty akers next plowing. She cant have it if lets Oscar live on it i want i should have it back if she does.

Tell mama that six hundret dollars she has been looking for ten years is berried from the bakhouse behind about ten feet down. She better let little Fredrick do the digging and count it when he comes up.

71

Mama should the rest get but i want it so that Adolph should tell her what not she should do so no more slick irishers sell her vaken cleaner they noise like hell and a broom don't cost so much.

I want it that mine brother Adolph be my executor and i want it that the judge should please make Adolph plenty bond put up and watch him like hell. Adolph is a good bisness man but only a dumpph would trust him with a busted pfennig.

Oscar don't nothing get. Tell Adolph he can have a hudret dollars if he prove to judge Oscar dont nothing get. That dam sure fix Oscar.

HERMAN OBERWEISS

—from *The Judicial Humorist*, edited by William L. Prosser, Little, Brown and Company, Boston.

★

Excerpts from the Last Will and Testament of the Marquis d'Aligre:

Article VII. I withdraw from N. A. ___ and N ___ the sum I had left them by a former will; they have so often proclaimed that I am a man who would cut a farthing in four, that I would on no account oblige - them to change their opinion. . . .

Article X. I leave 20,000 francs a year to the invalids who being on guard on the Pont des Arts in 1839, and judging from the shabbiness of my dress that I was in distress, paid for me the five centimes toll. . . .

Article XIV. I leave 200,000 francs a year to the "Phalansterians"; but they are only to receive this sum on the day on which they shall have transformed the ocean into orangeade . . .

Article XVI. Taking compassion on the poor of the first arrondissement, I desire that the value of the cereals harvested on my land at the next harvest shall be distributed to them in its entirety. . . .

Article XX. Finally, I leave to my relatives, oblivion; to my

"He makes out a new will every week.
Says he never had so much fun in his life."

friends, ingratitude; to God, my soul. As for my body, it belongs to my family vault. . . .

The Marquis concludes his will with this message to his family:

As for you, my relatives, who have been so long spelling upon this fortune, on which "I had concentrated all my affections," you are not going to touch a penny of it, and not one of you will be able to boast that you have squandered the millions which the old Marquis d'Aligre had taken so many years to hoard up.

★

Edward Wortley Montagu, son of the English ambassador to Turkey, signed and executed in 1716 a curious will, which was published with some important names merely hinted at. It reads, in part:

. . . to my noble and worthy relation, the Earl of ___ :I do not give his lordship any further part of my property because the best part of that he has contrived to take already.

Item. To Lord ___, I give nothing, because I know he'll bestow it on the poor.

Item. To ___, the author for putting me in his travels, I give five shillings for his wit, undeterred by the charge of extravagance, since friends who have read his book consider five shillings too much.

Item. To Sir Robert Walpole I leave my political opinions, never doubting he can well turn them into cash, who has always found such an excellent market in which to change his own.

Item. My cast-off habit of swearing oaths I give to Sir Leopold D ___, in consideration that no oaths have ever been able to find him yet.

★

IN THE NAME OF GOD, AMEN:

I, William Dunlop, of Gairbraid, in the township of Colburne, county and district of Huron, Western Canada, Esquire, being in sound health of body, and my mind just as usual (which my friends who flatter me say is no great shakes at the best of times), do make this my last will and testament as follows, revoking of course all former wills.

I leave the property of Gairbraid and all other landed property I may die possessed of to my sisters, Helen Boyle Story and Elizabeth Boyle Dunlop, the former because she is married to a minister whom (God help him) she henpecks; the latter because she is married to nobody nor is she like to be, for she is an old maid and not market rife. . . .

I leave my silver tankard to the eldest son of Old John, as the representative of the family. I would have left it to Old John himself, but he would melt it down and make temperance medals and that would be sacrilege.

I leave Parson Chavasse (Maggy's husband) the snuff box I got from the Sarnia Militia, as a small token of my gratitude for the service he has done the family in taking a sister that no man of taste would have taken.

I also give my late brother's watch to my brother Sandy, exhorting him at the same time to give up whiggery, radicalism and all other sins that do most beset him.

I leave John Caddle a silver tea-pot, the end that he may drink tea therefrom and comfort him under the affliction of a slatternly wife.

I leave my brother Alan my big silver snuff box, as I am informed he is a rather decent Christian with a swag belly and a jolly face. . . .

(signed) W. DUNLOP
August 31, 1842

★

Garvey B. White died in 1908. In his will he directed:

> . . . *that before anything else is done fifty cents be paid to my son-in-law to enable him to buy for himself a good stout rope with which to hang himself, and thus rid mankind of one of the most infamous scoundrels that ever roamed this broad land or dwelt outside of a penitentiary.*

A Variety of
Parchments

*He may make a will upon his nail for anything he
has to give.*

OLD PROVERB

Mr. Meeson's Will, a novel by Rider Haggard, tells of a
will tattooed on the back of the lovely heroine. This of course
was fiction, and even Rider Haggard fans found it difficult to
accept the fantastic tale. But in the following pages truth
comes up with some tall stories of its own.

Included among the "strange parchments" admitted to
probate in the United States were a will written on the back of
a bridge score card (Mrs. Charlotte N. Lawrence of Hemp-
stead, New York), a will written on the back of a visiting
card (Theodore G. Harris) and a will written on a prescription
blank (Dr. John H. Locke). M. Grant Hawkins, a Philadelphia resident who died insolvent, wrote his will on the back
of a dunning letter from a creditor.

★

A will probated in 1955 was written on a hatbox by a
factory worker. In it he left everything to his common-law
wife—*"my only friend."*

★

Otto G. Richter, who died in 1960, disposed of six million dollars by a will scrawled on a hospital chart.

★

The will of Frank C. Likas, probated April 26, 1955, was written on a paper doily at a table in an Oak Lawn, Illinois restaurant.

★

Mrs. Chleo Newman jotted down her will on the back of an envelope before starting off on an airplane trip in 1947. She wrote it in an airport restaurant before taking off (it was witnessed by a waitress) because "she had a premonition of disaster." The plane crashed over West Virginia, killing eighteen passengers, including Mrs. Newman.

Andrew Komlody's will, leaving all he possessed to his wife, was written in indelible pencil on the whitewashed wall of the Carteret, New Jersey, jail cell where he hung himself with strips made from his blanket. (It was Mrs. Komlody who had caused the arrest because, she said, her husband was jealous and making trouble.)

★

Mrs. Beth A. Baer, a blind woman, wrote out her will with a pen that ran out of ink. Handwriting expert Clark Sellers was able to make out the words from the indentations left on the paper by the pen. Mrs. Baer's "blank paper" will was filed for probate in the Los Angeles Superior Court on April 11, 1950.

*"The way everything has gone up, he might at
least have cut us off with five dollars!"*

Drawing by Tobey

★

The twenty-nine-word will of William Harold Taylor, probated in 1935, was written on the reverse side of a dance invitation. Some years before his death, as Mr. Taylor was setting out for Europe, a guest at his bon voyage party asked him if he had a will. Mr. Taylor drew the dance invitation from his pocket and wrote the will.

★

Mrs. Lorolina Nordquist, seventy-two, believing she was lost in the woods, wrote her will in green chalk on the wall of a shack where she sought shelter. Searchers found her will and located the unconscious woman on a mound of straw inside the shack. She later recovered.

★

In a world which seems sometimes to be drowning in paper, it is difficult to visualize the lack of a piece of paper when it is crucially needed. But, according to Lillian Pelkey and Madeline Higgins, nurses for the late George W. Hazeltine, such was the case when their dying patient suddenly decided to write his last will not too long ago.

Faced with a willing testator and a temporary paper shortage, the resourceful Miss Pelkey rose to the occasion. She pulled up her dress and offered Mr. Hazeltine a portion of her white petticoat on which to write his will—the bulk of his estate to a grandniece and ten thousand dollars each to Miss Pelkey and Miss Higgins as a reward for their devotion. Both women signed as witnesses.

"The Petticoat Will" was filed for probate in a Los Angeles court and the trial that ensued to determine the validity of the nurses' claim attracted national attention. The jury declared the will genuine but the judge ruled that it was null and void on a technicality: An individual named in a will cannot also act as a witness.

★

Entered for probate in 1913 and now residing with the register of wills, Philadelphia, Pennsylvania, is a page from a handwritten recipe book containing the will of Maggie Nothe.

Under the heading "Chili Sauce Without Working" appears the following:

4 quarts of ripe tomatoes, 4 small onions, 4 green peppers, 2 teacups of sugar, 2 quarts of cider vinegar, 2 ounces ground allspice, 2 ounces cloves, 2 ounces cinnamon, 12 teaspoonfuls salt. Chop tomatoes, onions and peppers fine, add the rest mixed together and bottle cold. Measure tomatoes when peeled. In case I die before my husband I leave everything to him.

(signed) MAGGIE NOTHE

★

Into the solemn atmosphere of an English court marched Maggie Barnes, widow of James Barnes, a canal pilot. In her hand she held an empty eggshell; on it was written with an indelible pencil in her husband's hand: *"Jan. 1925. Mag. Everything I Possess. J.B."*

This, claimed Maggie, was her husband's real Last Will, not the 1920 document which required that she share her late husband's eight-thousand-pound legacy with two stepsons.

When it was pointed out that an eggshell was a strange place for a will—and an unwitnessed will at that!—Maggie's attorney countered that this "document" should be considered a sailor's will executed at sea and therefore no witnesses were necessary.

Was this eggshell, inscribed by a canal boat pilot on the Manchester to Liverpool run, a "testamentary disposition by

"In view of my firm belief in reincarnation,
I do hereby direct that my entire estate be
held in trust, pending my return to this earth."

Drawing by Richter;
© The New Yorker Magazine, Inc.

a mariner at sea?" Lord Marivale, surrogate of the Probate Court, Manchester, ruled against the eggshell "will" and in favor of the earlier bequest written on a respectable sheet of paper and witnessed by three upstanding citizens.

★

Mine detectors, clairvoyants, a talking parakeet and an ocean-going bottle were all part of a frantic, fantastic search for a will that nobody was really sure ever existed. The prize was the fifteen-million-dollar estate of Daisy Alexander, the third daughter of sewing machine monarch Isaac Singer. Events following Mrs. Alexander's death in 1939 led from a stately mansion in London to a lonely beach five thousand miles away in San Francisco.

Although Mrs. Alexander promised her solicitor, Barry Cohen, that he would be generously provided for in the new will she had drawn, the only will found after her death was a thirty-year-old document which disposed of only a small portion of the vast estate to several distant relatives. Convinced that a later will existed and goaded by visions of a fifteen-million-dollar pot at the end of the rainbow, solicitor Cohen initiated a marathon search that would extend over several decades.

Following a fruitless exploration of Mrs. Alexander's Grosvernor Square mansion, a mine detector was moved in and a careful, painstaking probe made of every inch of the ceiling and walls in the hope of finding a safe or receptacle holding the missing document.

Newspaper accounts of the search brought in hundreds of suggestions—a woman from a Kentish County with a "vision," a real honest-to-goodness witch doctor, a cultist with a pendulum that stops when it locates the missing item—and finally, a full-fledged clairvoyant named Frederick Liston. Liston ran his fingers over a letter written by Mrs. Alexander and from "sympathetic vibrations" he received came up with some astonishingly accurate revelations of every phase of the dead woman's life—everything, that is, except the location of the elusive will.

One of the servants remembered that Mrs. Alexander spent many of her last days with a pet parakeet, Bob. According to the servants Bob was a fluent talker. The search party, with a covey of reporters at its heels, took off in pursuit of the bird who might be persuaded to drop a hint into Mr. Cohen's receptive ear. The bird was traced through three subsequent owners and when finally located was not only dead but ingloriously stuffed.

In 1947, on a deserted beach in San Francisco, Jack Wurm, an unemployed restaurant worker, picked up a bottle washed ashore by the tide. He broke the neck of the bottle, pulled out the scrap of paper inside and read:

To avoid confusion, I leave my entire estate to the lucky person who finds this bottle and to my attorney, Barry Cohen, share and share alike.

DAISY ALEXANDER
June 20, 1937

Daisy Alexander often threw bottles into the ocean wondering where they would go. When news of the find reached London, Daisy's friends said that putting a will in a bottle would be "just like her."

An expert on ocean currents testified that it would take a bottle approximately twelve years to make such a trip. Jack Wurm found the bottle eleven years and eight months after the date on the will.

Solicitor Cohen and his potential co-beneficiary Jack Wurm were, it would seem, close to the pot of gold at last —except for one important detail. To be honored in a British court a will must be witnessed, an embellishment sadly lacking in the scrap of paper washed ashore in San Francisco. The "will" is still floating through the courts, bobbing up now and again, but thirty nine years after Daisy Alexander's death, no settlement has been reached.

★

High up on a shelf, among hundreds of volumes of wills filed at the Surrogate Court in the District of Kerrobert, Canada, sits an unlikely "document"—a fender cut from a farm tractor. Its presence is explained by an accident that occurred at noon on June 8, 1948, when a tractor accidentally backed up, pinning George Harris beneath a disc apparatus he was adjusting. Mr. Harris' hands were free but the lower part of his leg was caught and bleeding profusely, making it impossible for him to free himself and reach help.

He was found in that position nine hours later and rushed to the hospital, where he died shortly after. One of the men examining the accident site a few days later noticed some writing scratched on the fender of Harris' tractor. It read:

In case I die in this mess, I leave all to the wife.
                              CECIL GEORGE HARRIS

Bits of fender were found on the knife in the dead man's pocket and it was obvious that he had used the knife to scratch the message while pinned beneath the machine. The fender was removed from the tractor, admitted to probate and filed with the registrar of wills as the Last Will and Testament of George Harris.

★

Informed by his doctor that he had only hours to live, Charles S. Orrin, a British businessman, wrote out his will in shorthand. The stenographic characters were so perfectly executed that the court reporter was able to read the document with ease and the will was admitted to probate without delay on August 7, 1922.

★

*"Now go out and get me a dog
named Rover!"*

Courtesy Larry Barth

Richard Brinkley's method of will forgery was almost too simple—it was destined to fail. At the bedside of old and ailing Mrs. Johanna Blume, he produced a piece of paper: Would Mrs. Blume like to join a small congenial group on a brief picnic in the country? If so, would she sign here please?

Mrs. Blume was, of course, not signing a picnic roster but her own will, neatly written out and hidden above the fold. Successful thus far, Brinkley repeated the ruse with two of his neighbors, whose signatures would serve as "witnesses" on the will.

When, shortly after, old Mrs. Blume passed away and Brinkley claimed her house and an eight-hundred-pound bank account under the terms of the will, the curiously folded sheet of paper was viewed with suspicion. Brinkley began to worry about what the witnesses would say. Having quickly concluded that their testimony could be troublesome, he resolved to get rid of the witnesses.

He called on the first witness, a Mr. Parket, and brought along a little gift—a bottle of oatmeal stout highly recommended for its restorative qualities. Mr. Parket never got to taste the stout, but his landlord, Richard Beck, and Beck's wife Elizabeth sneaked a large swallow while Parket was out of his room. Within minutes husband and wife died of convulsions from the effects of poisoning by prussic acid.

"Well, I'm sugared. That's very awkward, isn't it?" said Mr. Brinkley when he was arrested. Sugared he may have been, but hanged he was too—at Wandsworth Prison in England on August 13, 1907.

★

Any listing of strange will "parchments" must include the nonexistent parchment of Edward P. McNulty, entered to probate by Surrogate Wingate of Kings County, New York, on February 21, 1923.

Because the actual will had been torn up and thrown away by mistake by a nurse shortly after the death of the testator, Mrs. McNulty's brother, Martin Malone, entered the witness

"And to my brother George Clark, who was always telling me that 'health is more important than wealth,' I leave my rowing machine."

Courtesy Hank Ketcham

stand and described the contents of the will disposing of one hundred thousand dollars in real and personal property. (To do this he had to waive his right as a beneficiary.) Surrogate Wingate ruled that there had been a will and that the contents were as alleged.

★

The female sex, noted for its long goodbyes, will not easily upset the all-time world's record set by the late Mrs. Frederick Cook, the widow of a London drapery manufacturer. Her will, the longest on record, was admitted to probate on November 7, 1925. Its 95,940 words and 1,066 pages are contained in four bulky volumes (at 1925 prices, a copy of the will cost four hundred dollars).

Mrs. Cook left an estate valued at one hundred thousand dollars with instructions that her diary be burned and, once again reverting to womanly ways, a request that her age be omitted from the memorial stone.

★

The briefest, smallest will on record was written on the identification disc of a British soldier lost at sea. The complete text consisted of three words: *"All to mother."* It was scratched on the metal in characters so small that a microscope was needed to read the message.

Irving Trust Company of New York reports a similar three word will, *"All to mother."* In this case, however, there was a special problem: To whom did the will-writer refer? "Mother" was what he called both his wife and his parent.

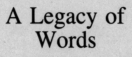

A Legacy of
Words

*"The idea of property, of something in common,
does not mix cordially with friendship, but
is inseparable from near relationship. We owe a
return in kind, where we feel no obligation
for a favour; and consign our possessions to our
next of kin as mechanically as we lean our
heads on the pillow, and go out of the world
in the same state of stupid amazement that
we came into it!"*

WILLIAM HAZLITT

"The Will of Charles Lounsberry," is a fictional bit of
prose by William Fish which first appeared in Harper's
Weekly in 1898. It has been reprinted frequently, quoted
often, and proved a boon over the years to the editor with
several inches of white space to fill and a deadline to meet.

Like the poster illustration which simply cries out for a
doodled mustache, a goatee and a pair of spectacles, the
"Lounsberry Will" invites the embellishment of editors and
rewrite men with a ready pencil who prefer "creek" to
"brook," "daisies" to "dandelions" and "forest" to "woods."

The author, in a Foreword to a privately printed edition,
tells of an editor who was so moved by the thought, "to boys
all streams and ponds where one may skate," that he added

the phrase, "when grim winter comes." Mr. Fish writes, "Some writers can boast that their works have been translated into all foreign languages, but when I look pathetically about for some little boast, I can only say that this one of my pieces has been translated into all the idiot tongues of English."

Besides playing fast and loose with the text, editors will attempt to give the piece an extra quiver of human interest by presenting it as a genuine will. Some quick surgery on the introductory paragraphs, and the will can be attributed to a penniless hobo who died on the streets of the Bowery—or a once-great poet who ended his days in a state penitentiary. As you can see, the romantic possibilities are endless.

"The Will of Charles Lounsberry" needs no embellishments or a hastily contrived testator to give it meaning. It stands by itself as a warm and sentimental piece of Americana—a legacy for all of us. This version, unchanged and unadorned, appears as it was first published in 1898.

"He was stronger and cleverer, no doubt, than other men, and in many broad lines of business he had grown rich, until his wealth exceeded exaggeration. One morning, in his office, he directed a request to his confidential lawyer to come to him in the afternoon—he intended to have his will drawn. A will is a solemn matter, even with men whose life is given up to business, and who are by habit mindful of the future. After giving this direction he took up no other matter, but sat at his desk alone and in silence.

"It was a day when summer was first new. The pale leaves upon the trees were starting forth upon the yet unbending branches. The grass in the parks had a freshness in its green like the freshness of the blue in the sky and of the yellow of the sun—a freshness to make one wish that life might renew its youth. The clear breezes from the south wantoned about, and then were still, as if loath to go finally away. Half idly, half thoughtfully, the rich man wrote upon the white paper before him, beginning what he wrote with capital letters,

such as he had not made since, as a boy in school, he had
taken pride in his skill with the pen:

In the Name of God, Amen

*I, CHARLES LOUNSBERRY, being of sound and dispos-
ing mind and memory (he lingered on the word memory), do
now make and publish this my last will and testament, in
order, as justly as I may, to distribute my interests in the
world among succeeding men.*

*And first, that part of my interests which is known among
men and recognized in the sheepbound volumes of the law as
my property, being inconsiderable and of none account, I
make no account of in this my will.*

*My right to live, it being but a life estate, is not at my
disposal, but, these things excepted, all else in the world I
now proceed to devise and bequeath.*

*ITEM: And first, I give to good fathers and mothers, but in
trust for their children, nevertheless, all good little words of
praise and all quaint pet names, and I charge said parents to
use them justly, but generously, as the needs of their children
shall require.*

*ITEM: I leave to children exclusively, but only for the life
of their childhood, all and every the dandelions of the fields
and the daisies thereof, with the right to play among them
freely, according to the custom of children, warning them at
the same time against the thistles. And I devise to children the
yellow shores of creeks and the golden sands beneath the
waters thereof, with the dragon-flies that skim the surface of
said waters, and the odors of the willows that dip into said
waters, and the white clouds that float high over the giant
trees.*

*And I leave to children the long, long days to be merry in,
in a thousand ways, and the Night and the Moon and the
train of the Milky Way to wonder at, but subject, nevertheless, to the rights hereinafter given to lovers; and I give to
each child the right to choose a star that shall be his, and I
direct that the child's father shall tell him the name of it, in*

order that the child shall always remember the name of that star after he has learned and forgotten astronomy.

ITEM: I devise to boys jointly all the useful idle fields and commons where ball may be played, and all snow-clad hills where one may coast, and all streams and ponds where one may skate, to have and to hold the same for the period of their boyhood. And all meadows, with the clover blooms and butterflies thereof; and all woods, with their appurtenances of squirrels and whirring birds and echoes and strange noises; and all distant places which may be visited, together with the adventures there found, I do give to said boys to be theirs. And I give to said boys each his own place at the fireside at night, with all pictures that may be seen in the burning wood or coal, to enjoy without let or hindrance and without any incumbrance of cares.

ITEM: To lovers I devise their imaginary world, with whatever they may need, as the stars of the sky, the red, red roses by the wall, the snow of the hawthorn, the sweet strains of music, or aught else they may desire to figure to each other the lastingness and beauty of their love.

ITEM: To young men jointly, being joined in a brave, mad crowd, I devise and bequeath all boisterous, inspiring sports of rivalry. I give to them the disdain of weakness and undaunted confidence in their own strength. Though they are rude and rough, I leave to them alone the power of making lasting friendships and of possessing companions, and to them exclusively I give all merry songs and brave choruses to sing, with smooth voices to troll them forth.

ITEM: And to those who are no longer children, or youths, or lovers, I leave Memory, and I leave to them the volumes of the poems of Burns and Shakespeare, and of other poets, if there are others, to the end that they may live the old days over again freely and fully, without tithe or diminution; and to those who are no longer children, or youths, or lovers, I leave, too, the knowledge of what a rare, rare world it is."

★

After the endless accounts of wills for the benefit of animals here's a switch—the will of a dog. A distinguished dog but a dog nevertheless. "Blemie's will" was written by America's great playwright Eugene O'Neill just before his beloved pet died of old age. O'Neill wrote it to comfort his wife Carlotta and prepare her for Blemie's passing. First printed for private distribution it was later reprinted in "Look" magazine.

I, Silverdene Emblem O'Neill (familiarly known to my family, friends and acquaintances as Blemie), because the burden of my years and infirmities is heavy upon me, and I realize the end of my life is near, do hereby bury my last will and testament in the mind of my Master. He will not know it is there until after I am dead. Then, remembering me in his loneliness, he will suddenly know of this treatment, and I ask him then to inscribe it as a memorial to me.

I have little in the way of material things to leave. Dogs are wiser than men. They do not set great store upon things. They do not waste their days hoarding property. They do not ruin their sleep worrying about how to keep the objects they have not. There is nothing of value I have to bequeath except my love and my faith. These I leave to all those who have loved me, to my Master and Mistress, who I know will mourn me most, to Freeman who has been so good to me, to Cyn and Roy and Willie and Naomi and— But if I should list all those who have loved me it would force my Master to write a book. Perhaps it is vain of me to boast when I am so near death, which returns all beasts and vanities to dust, but I have always been an extremely lovable dog.

I ask my Master and Mistress to remember me always, but not to grieve for me too long. In my life I have tried to be a comfort to them in time of sorrow, and a reason for added joy in their happiness. It is painful for me to think that even in death I should cause them pain. Let them remember that while no dog has ever had a happier life (and this I owe to their love and care for me), now that I have grown blind and deaf and lame, and even my sense of smell fails me so that a rabbit could be right under my nose and I might not know, my pride has sunk to a sick, bewildered humiliation. I feel life is taunting me with having over-lingered my welcome. It is time I said goodbye, before I become too sick a burden on myself and on those who love me. It will be sorrow to leave them, but not a sorrow to die. Dogs do not fear death as men do. We accept it as part of life, not as something alien and terrible which destroys life. What may come after death, who knows? I would like to believe with those of my fellow Dalmatians who are devout Mohammedans, that there is a Paradise where one is always young and full-bladdered; where all the day one dillies and dallies with an amorous multitude of houris, beautifully spotted; where jack rabbits that run fast but not too fast (like the houris) are as the sands of the desert; where each blissful hour is mealtime; where in long evenings there are a million fireplaces with logs forever burning, and one curls oneself up and blinks into the flames and nods and dreams, remembering the old brave days on earth, and the love of one's Master and Mistress.

I am afraid this is too much for even such a dog as I am to expect. But peace, at least, is certain. Peace and long rest for weary old heart and head and limbs, and eternal sleep in the earth I have loved so well. Perhaps, after all, this is best.

One last request I earnestly make. I have heard my Mistress say, "When Blemie dies we must never have another dog. I love him so much I could never love another one." Now I would ask her, for love of me, to have another. It would be a poor tribute to my memory never to have a dog again. What I would like to feel is that, having once had me in the family, now she cannot live without a dog! I have never had a narrow jealous spirit. I have always held that most dogs are good (and one cat, the black one I have permitted to share the living room rug during the evenings, whose affection I have tolerated in a kindly spirit, and in rare sentimental moods, even reciprocated a trifle). Some dogs, of course, are better than others. Dalmatians, naturally, as everyone knows, are best. So I suggest a Dalmatian as my successor. He can hardly be as well bred or as well mannered or as distinguished and handsome as I was in my prime. My Master and Mistress must not ask the impossible. But he will do his best, I am sure, and even his inevitable defects will help by comparison to keep my memory green. To him I bequeath my collar and leash and my overcoat and raincoat, made to order in 1929 at Hermes in Paris. He can never wear them with the distinction I did, walking around the Place Vendôme, or later along Park Avenue, all eyes fixed on me in admiration; but again I am sure he will do his utmost not to appear a mere gauche provincial dog. Here on the ranch, he may prove himself quite worthy of comparison, in some respects. He will, I presume, come closer to jack rabbits than I have been able to in recent years. And, for all his faults, I hereby wish him the happiness I know will be his in my old home.

One last word of farewell, Dear Master and Mistress. Whenever you visit my grave, say to yourselves with regret but also with happiness in your hearts at the remembrance of my long happy life with you: "Here lies one who loved us and whom we loved." No matter how deep my sleep I shall hear you, and not all the power of death can keep my spirit from wagging a grateful tail.

Tao House, December 17th, 1940.

★

Excerpts from "The Green Bag," a law review published early in this century . . .

"Where would the novelist of the period be without the disinheriting will, the manipulated will, the secreted will, and all kinds of wills in every style of obliteration and in

every stage of destruction? Why he would be nearly as bereft of staple stock in trade as if he had lost the lovelorn maiden, the tender-hearted soldier, or the grand old hall of our ancestors. Even writers of a higher grade find it convenient to make use of such machinery to help make the story go."

★

"Not long ago a Boston man died, whose will left his wife penniless unless she married again within five years, the reason given for this proviso being that he wanted somebody else to find out how hard it was to live with her—truly a monstrous revelation of post-mortem spite, and one that any decent court ought to set aside.

"But such wills are rare; it is much more common to find testamentary provisions against wives marrying again. If report speaks truly, such prohibitions do not always strike the grief-stricken widow as wise or proper."

★

"There is a tendency in England, on the part of engaged men, to draw up wills in favor of the ladies to whom they are engaged. By thus anticipating what they would truly do after marriage, they not only take duty by the forelock, so to speak, but reap a present reward in the increased ardor of the adored one."

★

"If a way to take it with you is ever
discovered, he reserves the right to come
back for his."

Conditional Wills

"Let's choose executors and talk of wills."

SHAKESPEARE
RICHARD II

To a man accustomed to purchasing obedience for cash the mere incidence of his death need not be a handicap. Not as long as he can write a will setting forth the conditions that must be met or the benefits withheld. Projecting his authority beyond the grave, the will-maker gets a final chance to pay the piper and call the tune.

For example, a rector of a Yorkshire parish, who died in 1804 (roughly 150 years before the advent of the bikini), left a substantial sum to his daughter with this proviso:

Seeing that my daughter Anna has not availed herself of my advice touching the objectionable practice of going about with her arms bare up to the elbows, my will is that, should she continue after my death in this violation of the modesty of her sex, all the goods, chattels, moneys, land, and other that I have devised to her for the maintenance of her future life shall pass to the oldest of the sons of my sister Caroline.

Should anyone take exception to this my wish as being too severe, I answer that license in dress in a woman is a mark of a depraved mind.

107

The way the rector felt about bare arms, James Fleming felt about mustaches. Mr. Fleming, the owner of a large and thriving furniture factory, was a charitable man, a man who didn't have very strong feelings about anything—except mustaches, the sight of which he despised.

When he died in 1869, he left a will stipulating that each man in his employ was to receive ten pounds, providing he did not wear a mustache. Being a generous man, he could not bring himself to cut off his mustached employees without a cent. They were to receive five pounds each.

★

A Californian named John Quincy Murray, who died in 1929, gave three thousand dollars to two granddaughters on condition that they give up bobbed hair, rouge and powder, jewelry, dances and movies, and that they wear their dresses *"long at both ends."*

He also left a thousand dollars to his grandson provided he would forgo dances and motion pictures and that he would never grow a mustache.

★

Obviously, it is not possible to be passive about mustaches. You either like them or you don't. Henry Budd, a prosperous shipbuilder who died in 1862, was another who didn't like mustaches and said so in his will:

In case my son Edward shall wear a mustache, then the devise hereinbefore contained in favor of him, his appointees, heirs and assigns of my said estate, called Pepper Park, shall be void; and I devise the same estate to my son William, his appointees, heirs and assigns. And in case my son William shall wear a mustache, then the devise hereinbefore contained in favor of him, his appointees, heirs, assigns of my said estate called Twickinham Park, shall be void; and I devise the said estate of my son Edward, his appointees, heirs and assigns. And in case my son Edward . . .

★

A Vienna banker making a large bequest of property and cash to his nephew stipulated that *"he shall never, on any occasion, read a newspaper, his favorite occupation."*

★

Nephews seem to be the favorite target of capricious millionaires. An exceedingly wealthy Englishman named Sergeant, who died without sons, left each of his nephews sizeable annuities, with a string attached:

As my nephews are fond of indulging themselves in bed in the morning, and as I wish them to prove to the satisfaction of my executors that they have got out of bed in the morning, and either employed themselves in business or taken exercise in the open air, from five to eight o'clock every morning from the fifth of April to the tenth of October, being three hours each day, and from seven to nine o'clock in the morning from the tenth of October to the fifth of April, being two hours every evening; this is to be done for some years, during the first seven years to the satisfaction of my executors, who may excuse them in case of illness, but the task must be made up when they are well, and if they will not do this, they shall not receive any share of my property. Temperance makes the faculties clear, and exercise makes them vigorous.

★

When he died in 1933, John D. Morgan of Elizabeth, New Jersey, left two million dollars but took with him the financial acumen that built so vast an estate. In recognition of this fact, Mr. Morgan stipulated in his will that his two daughters must first pass an examination on the "principles of sound investment" in order to qualify for the bequest. The will states that:

> . . . they each thoroughly satisfy the trustees that they understand the principles of sound investment substantially as they are explained in some standard authoritative work on this subject; this examination must show that they have a practical knowledge of such principles, permanently understood and remembered, and not a mere temporary committing to memory of some book.

★

Billy Rose, the bantam-size showman turned financial wizard—when he died he was the largest individual holder of A.T. & T. stock—left a carefully constructed and well-written will plus an estate worth from $25 to $30 million but it was some time before he could rest in peace. Billy was kept in a cold storage vault for two years while his two sisters fought with the executors of the estate on the cost of the Billy Rose mausoleum and went to court to break the will. It was finally agreed that Billy would be buried in a mausoleum on a plot of land large enough to hold eighty coffins.

The Napoleon complex survives the grave.

★

When he died in 1953, McNair Ilgenfritz left the Metropolitan Opera $150,000, the score for an opera that he composed and the condition that if the Met wanted the money it must also take the opera.

For a while it looked as if Mr. Ilgenfritz would realize posthumously a goal that eluded him during his lifetime. The bequest came at a time when the Metropolitan was having more than its usual financial problems, and serious consideration was given to accepting the conditions set forth in the will and presenting the late composer's work at the revered opera house. In the midst of mounting criticism that art was being

110

"This is the Last Will and Testament of Elias
M. Pinzer, dentist. This is going to hurt
a little . . ."

compromised and the institution "bought off," the bequest was refused.

Mr. Ilgenfritz's opera was never produced at the Metropolitan Opera.

★

In 1957, Mrs. Viola Laski was left an inheritance of $325,000. According to the conditions of her mother's will she must live in the U.S. or be *"physically present"* at the *quarterly distribution of interest.*

Said British subject Mrs. Laski: "I shall forgo the money."

Husbands
and Wives

The comfortable estate of widowhood is the only hope that keeps up a wife's spirits.

JOHN GAY,
The Beggar's Opera

A French merchant who died in the year 1610 left a handsome legacy to a lady who had refused to marry him twenty years before. He did so, he said in his will, to express his gratitude for "a happy bachelor life of independence and freedom."

Not everyone is that fortunate. Instead of a rejection many a man has found himself a short-term winner and a long-term loser: she said "yes" and he lived unhappily ever after. Then, after years of misery, the aggrieved husband finds, at last, the perfect device with which to strike back. Through his will he hopes to have the last word even if it means reaching out from beyond the grave to do so.

Such a man was John Packer, a wealthy bookseller living at Old Bond Street, London until his death in 1791.

To one Elizabeth Packer, whom through fondness I made my wife, without regard to family, fame and fortune, and who in return has not spared most unjustly to accuse me of every

115

*crime regarding human nature, except highway robbery, I
bequeath fifty pounds.*

★

Excerpt from the will of Henry, Earl of Stafford (seventeenth century):

*I give to the worst of women, who is guilty of all ills—the
daughter of Mr. Gramont, a Frenchman—whom I have
unfortunately married, five and forty brass halfpence, which
will buy her a pullet for her supper—a greater sum than her
father can often make over to her—for I have known when he
had neither money nor credit for such a purchase, he being
the worst of men, and his wife the worst of women in all
debaucheries.*

★

Colonel Charles Nash, who died at the end of the nineteenth century, bequeathed an annuity of fifty pounds to the
bell ringers of Bath Abbey, England, on the condition that
they muffle the clappers of the bells and *"ring them with
doleful accentuation"* from 8 a.m. to 8 p.m. on each
anniversary of his wedding day and, during the same hours,
"with a merry peal" on the anniversary of the day in which
death released him from the tyranny of domestic togetherness.

★

John George of Lambeth died in London in June 1791. His
wife not only drove him to distraction but to the heights of
eloquence:

*Seeing that I have had the misfortune to be married to the
aforesaid Elizabeth, who, ever since our union, has tormented me in every possible way; that not content with*

"I am reading it right. He left his money to
Johns Hopkins and his brain to you!"

making game of all my remonstrances, she has had done all she could to render my life miserable; that Heaven seems to have sent her into the world solely to drive me out of it; that the strength of Samson, the genius of Homer, the prudence of Augustus, the skill of Pyrrhus, the patience of Job, the philosophy of Socrates, the subtlety of Hannibal, the vigilance of Hermogenes, would not suffice to subdue the perversity of her charactor; that no power on earth can change her, seeing we have lived apart during the last eight years, and that the only result has been the ruin of my son, whom she has corrupted and estranged from me; weighing maturely and seriously all these considerations, I have bequeathed and I bequeath, to my said wife Elizabeth, the sum of one shilling, to be paid unto her within six months of my death.

★

What other men before and after him have tried to say, an anonymous New Jersey testator said with less words and more art. Until a better one comes to light, it remains the epitome of succinct vituperation:

"To my wife Anna (who is no damn good) I leave $1."

★

Pablo Picasso left an estimated $90,000,000 in bank accounts, investments, real estate . . . and an incalculable treasure of his own art. Picasso predicted that his heirs would quarrel and tear away at his fortune—"It will be worse than anyone can imagine"—and didn't bother to write a will. His second wife Jacqueline, his son Paulo and the two illegitimate children by the artist's former mistress Francoise Gilet (now Mrs. Jonas Salk) are still vying for larger shares of Picasso's huge estate.

★

118

An eighteen page will that Aristotle Socrates Onassis wrote on an airplane enroute from Acapulco to N.Y. made his daughter Christine Onassis one of the richest women in the world.

More than half of the Onassis fortune however, went to establish a foundation to further the arts, sciences and religion through competition and awards. It was an expression of the aging tycoon's collapsed dream. The foundation is dedicated to the memory of his son Alexander, who died at the age of 24 in an airplane crash.

Public interest in the will focused on how it treated the widow, Jacqueline Kennedy Onassis. Despite reports of a disintegrating marriage, the will made it clear that Onassis did not want to deprive Jackie of her Tiffany charge account. The document states that Jackie had renounced her legal rights (under Greek law up to 20 percent of the fortune) in exchange for a prenuptial agreement in which she received three million dollars in tax free bonds. In addition, under the terms of the will Jackie would receive a lifetime income of $250,000 annually, $50,000 a year for her two children by John F. Kennedy, 25 percent interest in the yacht and the Onassis-owned island, Skorpios.

The animosity between the daughter and the glamorous stepmother which was a matter of public knowledge during the last years of the Greek tycoon's life, grew even more intense after his death. When Christina contested the will to get a larger share of the fortune Jackie saw this action as a release from her prenuptial arrangement and opted for a larger claim. An army of lawyers were put to work for a year on the negotiations. To avoid any further repercussions Christina finally settled the claim: Jackie received a respectable $20 million plus $6 million to cover some of the taxes on the payoff.

★

Many men will find a bold champion in the person of William Durley. His will, filed in the nineteenth century, reads:

To my wife, Mary, one shilling, in recompence of her having picked my pocket of sixty guineas, and taken up money in my name, without my leave or license.

Mr. Durley's countryman John Davis cut his wife off with five shillings:

It is sufficient to enable her to get drunk for the last time at my expense.

Angry husbands may sympathize with these avenged testators of yesteryear but it is not possible for them to do likewise. The laws of all the states in the U.S., Great Britain and many other countries set a minimum share of the estate which a widow is entitled to if she contests the will and claims her "dower rights."

★

Any schoolboy can repeat Patrick Henry's stirring "give me liberty or give me death," but few people indeed are aware of the patriot's attitude on widow's rights. After making generous provisions in his will for his wife and children, Patrick Henry declares:

But in case my said wife shall marry again, in that case I revoke and make void every gift, legacy, authority, or power herein mentioned and order, will and direct, she, my said Wife, shall have no more of my estate than she can recover by Law; nor shall she be Guardian to any of my children, or Executrix of this my Will.

" . . . and to my sister, Emma Bentley, who
often said she would bet a hundred dollars that
a bunch of chorus girls would get my money, I
leave one hundred dollars."

Courtesy Hank Ketcham

Like her late husband, Dorothea Henry counted freedom of action above security. Disregarding the penalty, she remarried, taking as her new spouse Judge Edmund Winston, who was Patrick Henry's cousin.

★

Late in life, Gouverneur Morris, the celebrated orator and New York statesman, married Miss Ann Randolph, a lady much younger than himself. In appreciation of their short, happy life together, Gouverneur Morris bequeathed a handsome income to his young widow, providing in his will that in the event that she remarried the income should be doubled.

★

In one of the most remarkable bequests on record, Mrs. Robert C. Hayes, of Binghamton, New York, left her husband Robert—a new wife. The bride was Annamae, Mrs. Hayes' eldest daughter by a previous marriage.

The testator, who died in December of 1920, sought in a single stroke to promote the future happiness of her young husband and her divorced daughter. She left instructions that the two were to be married after her death and that the marriage ceremony was to take place within five days of her funeral.

Mrs. Hayes was buried on Wednesday. The following Monday, the recently widowed Robert Hayes, thirty-five, and his stepdaughter Annamae, twenty-one, were married.

★

The German poet Heinrich Heine left a will giving his wife all his assets, with one condition—that she remarry. *"Because,"* he says in his will, *"then there will be at least one man to regret my death."*

★

It was Mormon leader Brigham Young's rare experience to write a will for the distribution of his estate among seventeen wives and forty-eight children. The will, disposing of two and a half million dollars in cash and property, divides the families into "classes," each class being represented by a wife and children, or a wife without children or the children of a deceased wife. The Mormon prophet was also "sealed" to a number of other women, in accordance with the ritual of the Mormon Church, but there is no accurate count of this category and no mention is made of them in his will. Brigham Young drew on his considerable experience in the subject and stated in his will just what he meant by "a wife":

To avoid any question, the words married or marriage in this will shall be taken to have become consummated between man and woman, either by ceremony before a lawful magistrate or according to the order of the Church of Jesus Christ of Latter-Day Saints, or by their cohabitation in conformity to our custom.

★

Curiosities of the Search Room, a book published in England in 1880, records this nineteenth-century will:

As to all my worldly goods now, or to be, in store,
I give to my beloved wife, and hers for evermore.
I give all freely, I no limit fix:
This is my will, and she's executrix.

Unlike the poet who conceived it, this bit of verse has many lives. The same will, word for word, was admitted to probate in Newark on May 13, 1921 (Frederick E. Castle), in Bronx County on May 30, 1925 (Morris Deitsch) and twenty-one years later, on May 16, 1946, in Edgar County Court (John W. Maughmer). It is unlikely that collectors of odd wills have seen the last of it.

123

★

The three-page will of William Shakespeare—probably the most famous will in existence—is preserved in an airtight frame of thick glass and polished oak. This priceless document is kept in Somerset House, London, along with the wills of such luminaries as Samuel Johnson, Lord Nelson, William Pitt, Isaak Walton, the Duke of Wellington and John Milton.

Within the formal, legalistic language of Shakespeare's will, one provocative line catches the eye of the curious reader: *"Item: I give unto my wife my second best bed . . ."*

Is this confirmation of an unhappy married life—or a sentimental bequest motivated by love?

Many scholars and historians explain that "the second best bed" was the one associated with the couple's domestic life and so, rather than a personal slight, it was a romantic, thoughtful bequest. Others are not so sure. They point out that it was the custom during Shakespeare's time for men to mention their wives in their wills with high praise and terms of endearment. Not only was this missing in the Bard's will but even the modest bequest of the "second best bed" was an interlineation—an afterthought hastily scribbled in.

Those who look to Shakespeare's will to provide clues to the true relationship between Anne Hathaway and William Shakespeare must conclude that it only adds to the mystery.

Facsimile of part of nine lines
at the end of Shakespeare's will,
with his signature

A Sense of History

> *The tongues of dying men*
> *Enforce attention like deep harmony . . .*

SHAKESPEARE, Richard II

While directing the excavations at Kahun, British archaeologist Sir William Petrie unearthed a bit of papyrus folded vertically and sealed with a scarabaeus, a large black beetle regarded by ancient Egyptians as symbolic of resurrection and immortality. Translation by an Oxford scholar revealed the Last Will of Uah, dating back to some time around 1799 B.C. The will is a model of simplicity and clarity.

I, Uah, am giving a title to property to my wife Sheftu, the woman of Gesab who is called Teta, the daughter of Sat Sepdu, of all things given to me by my brother Ankh-ren. She shall give it to any she desires of her children she bears me.

I am giving to her the Eastern slaves, four persons, that my brother Ankh-ren gave me. She shall give them to whomsoever she will of her children.

As to my tomb, let me be buried in it with my wife alone.

Moreover, as to the house built for me by my brother, Ankh-ren, my wife shall dwell therein without allowing her to be put forth on the ground by any person.

Done in the presence of these witnesses. Kemen, decora-

*tor of columns. Apu, doorkeeper of the Temple. Senb, son of
Senb, doorkeeper of the Temple.*

★

*King's son Nek'ure makes the following command while
living upon his two feet and not ailing in any respect.*

The remainder of this will, carved on the wall of a tomb
some time around the year 2601 B.C., is barely decipherable.
In it, Nek'ure, son of the pharaoh King Khafre, disposes of
fourteen towns and two estates in the pyramid city created by
his father. The property was to be divided among his wife,
three children and an unknown person, possibly his mistress.

Fragments of the carving containing Nek'ure's will, the
oldest known to exist, can be found in the Berlin Museum.

★

The oldest will in the United States is filed at the
courthouse in Lancaster County, Virginia. It is the will of
Epraphrodibus Lawson of Rappahannock, Virginia, dated
March 31, 1652.

★

South African empire-builder Cecil Rhodes was obsessed
with wills. The first of his six wills, written when he was a
twenty-four-year-old undergraduate at Oxford, set the theme
that he would return to again and again:

> *. . . to and for the establishment, promotion and devel-
> opment of a Secret Society, the true aim and object whereof
> shall be the extension of British rule throughout the world,
> . . . the ultimate recovery of the United States of America
> as an integral part of the British Empire . . . and, finally,
> the foundation of so great a Power as hereafter to render
> wars impossible and promote the best interest of humanity.*

The next four wills contained variations of the Rhodesian manifesto for British domination of the world. However, when he drafted his sixth and last will, Rhodes perhaps sensed that this was to be the one that mattered, for he put aside his grandiose schemes and settled for reality. The essence of the will, as the world knows it, is the section which created the famous Rhodes Scholarships.

In the person of the Rhodes Scholar, a young man from either Britain, the U.S. or Germany, lies Cecil Rhodes' hope of Anglo-Saxon supremacy in the world.

★

With these words, Alfred Nobel, inventor of dynamite and nitroglycerine, established the most important prizes for achievement, the most sought-after distinction, anywhere in the world:

The whole of my remaining estate shall be dealt with in the following way: The capital shall be invested by my executors in safe securities and shall constitute a fund, the interest on which shall be annually distributed in the form of prizes to those who, during the preceding year, shall have conferred the greatest benefit on mankind.

The said interest shall be divided into five parts, which shall be apportioned as follows: one part to the person who shall have made the most important discovery or invention within the field of physics; one part to the person who shall have made the most important chemical discovery or improvement; one part to the person who shall have made the most important discovery within the domain of physiology or medicine; one part to the person who shall have produced in the field of literature the most outstanding work of an idealistic tendency; and one part to the person who shall have done the most or the best work for fraternity among nations, for the abolition or reduction of standing armies and for the holding and promotion of peace congresses.

It is my express wish that in awarding the prizes no consideration whatever shall be given to the nationality of the candidate, so that the most worthy shall receive the prize whether he be a Scandinavian or not.
Paris, November 27, 1895 ALFRED BERNHARD NOBEL

Events since the first Nobel Peace Prize was awarded provide an ironic footnote to Nobel's Last Will and Testament. The awards were continued all through the First World War but in 1940 they were suspended as the world waged the greatest war in history. The factories on both sides that fed ammunition to the conflicting forces were descendants of the original Nobel Explosive Company. The prizes were restored in 1943.

★

The will of Peter I (Czar of Russia from 1696 to 1725) presents a blueprint for the Russian domination of Europe. Although written more than two centuries ago, it has a familiar ring:

God, from whom we derive our existence, and to whom we owe our crown, having constantly enlightened us by his Spirit, and sustained us by his divine help, allows me to look on the Russian people as called upon hereafter to hold sway over Europe!

I found Russia as a rivulet: I leave it a river; my successors will make it a large sea, destined to fertilize the impoverished lands of Europe; and its waters will overflow, in spite of opposing dams, erected by weak hands.

1. Keep the Russian nation in a state of continual war, so as to have the soldier always under arms, and ready for action, excepting when the finances of the state will not allow it. Keep up the forces; choose the best moment for attack. By this means you will be ready for war even in the time of peace. This is for the interest of the future aggrandizement of Russia.

II. Endeavor, by every possible means, to bring in, from the neighboring civilized countries of Europe, officers in times of war, and learned men in times of peace, thus giving the Russian people the advantages enjoyed by other countries, without allowing them to lose any of their own self-respect.

III. On every occasion take a part in the affairs and quarrels of Europe: above all, in . . . Germany . . .

One section of Peter the Great's will was particularly prescient of current events in the explosive Middle East. In it he advised future Russian leaders . . .

Approach as near as possible to Constantinople [now Istanbul] and India. Whoever governs there will be the true sovereign of the world. Consequently, excite continual wars, not only in Turkey but in Persia [now Iran]. Establish dockyards in the Black Sea . . . In the decadence of Persia, penetrate as far as the Persian Gulf, reestablish if it be possible the ancient commerce with the Levant [the collective name for the countries on the Eastern shore of the Mediterranean from Egypt, Israel, Lebanon, Syria—up to and including Turkey], advance as far as India which is the depot of the world. Arrived at this point, we shall no longer have need of England's gold.

The above, together with a detailed plan of strategy, constitutes the Last Will and Testament of Peter the Great. Seven years after it was written George Washington was born.

★

From the Last Will and Testament of Napoleon, written on April 15, 1821 at St. Helena, the first five items:

1. I die in the apostolical Roman religion, in the bosom of which I was born, more than fifty years since.

2. It is my wish that my ashes may repose on the banks of

the Seine, in the midst of the French people, whom I have loved so well.

3. I have always had reason to be pleased with my dearest wife, Marie Louise. I retain for her to my last moment, the most tender sentiments—I beseech her to watch, in order to preserve my son from the snares which yet environ his infancy.

4. I recommend to my son, never to forget that he was born a French prince, and never to allow himself to become an instrument in the hands of the triumvirs who oppress the nations of Europe; he ought never to fight against France, or to injure her in any manner; he ought to adopt my motto —"Everything for the French people."

5. I die prematurely, assassinated by the English oligarchy. . . . The English nation will not be slow in avenging me.

★

"Now," said a French wit shortly after the fall of Napoleon, "there are only three great powers left: England, Russia and Madame de Staël."

Volumes have been written about Madame de Staël, the tempestuous, many-faceted and complex personality who dominated her time, but in the brief space of a single paragraph excerpted from her will, we learn what really made the lady tick—

"I commend my soul to God, Who has lavished His gifts on me in this world and Who has given me a father to whom I owe what I am and what I have, a father who would have saved me from all my errors if I had never turned away from his principles. I have but one counsel to give my children, and this is to have ever present in their minds the conduct, the virtues, and the talents of my father, and to imitate him, each according to his calling and his strength. I have known no one in this world who equaled my father, and every day

my respect and love for him become engraved more deeply on my heart."

★

The case of Myra Gaines Clark is by all odds the most remarkable case involving a will ever to be tried in American courts. The struggle to capture the thirty-million-dollar estate of Daniel Clark raged in the law courts for fifty years, appearing on ten separate occasions before the United States Supreme Court. Among the thirty lawyers who worked on the case were such luminaries as Daniel Webster, Reverdy Johnson and Francis Scott Key.

When Daniel Clark died in 1825, a will was filed which left the estate to Clark's elderly mother. Myra Gaines, his daughter, claimed that this will was fraudulent, that her father wrote a later will in 1813 leaving the estate to her.

Where was the 1813 will? According to Mrs. Gaines, it had been lost, stolen or destroyed—but, said she, such a will did at one time exist and she had a witness who had read it while her father was still alive.

Mrs. Gaines had to prove more than the existence of a will: She had to prove that, contrary to general belief, her parents were legally married. Unless she could prove her own legitimacy she could not inherit in Louisiana, where the Roman Code system of law is in force.

Although the fortune was vast, more than money was at stake. Mrs. Gaines was fighting for her mother's honor and for her own good name and it was this element of the case that captured the sympathy and interest of millions. Through fifty tempestuous years of American history, the slight figure of a woman pitted against impossible odds never left the public scene.

Defeated in New Orleans, Mrs. Gaines pressed her case in the federal courts. Defeated in the Supreme Court, Mrs. Gaines hired a new lawyer and began again. Forty years after her father's death, the Supreme Court acknowledged the existence of the will and accepted the testimony that a marriage did take place. The case was won but the benefits were still unrealized. It was 1864 and the nation was split in two by the Civil War. According to the rules of the confederacy, "any judgment rendered by a court of the United States shall be null and void in any seceded state."

After the war the legal cudgels were picked up and victory came once again, but by then the potentially richest woman in the United States was too old to care and too tired to pursue her claim. On January 1, 1885, after half a century of fighting, Myra Gaines Clark, old and in debt, died in a poorly furnished upstairs rented room.

★

From the will of Benjamin Franklin:

To my son William Franklin, late Governor of the Jerseys, I give and devise all the lands I hold or have a right to in the Province of Nova Scotia, to hold to him, his heirs and assigns forever. I also give him all my books and papers which he has in his possession, and all debts standing against him on my account books, willing that no payment for restitution of the same be required of him by my Executors. The part he acted against me in the late war, which is of public notoriety, will account for my leaving him no more of an estate he endeavored to deprive me of.

In contrast to the bitterness displayed toward his son, Franklin showered gifts and affection on his daughter Sarah and her husband Richard Bache.

"I wish to be useful even after my Death, if possible," wrote Franklin, and to this end he left one thousand pounds each to the cities of Philadelphia and Boston to be loaned out to young artisans after they had served their apprenticeship. The apprenticeship system has all but vanished from the American scene and much of the money set aside for helping young apprentices to get started has been redirected. Many

"You're missing a lot of fun by
sticking to one will!"

Drawing by Skiles

millions of dollars for charity and public works were generated by Franklin's original two-thousand-pound gift.

Franklin's will also includes this bequest:

My fine crabtree walking stick with a gold head, curiously wrought in the form of the cap of liberty, I give to my friend, and the friend of mankind, George Washington.

If it was a sceptre, he has merited and would become it.

We shall follow the walking stick with a gold head as it passes through the will of Washington.

★

George Washington's lengthy will begins by disposing of his estate to Martha Washington *("my dearly beloved wife")* and continues with this expression of Washington's wishes for the destiny of his slaves:

Upon the decease of my wife, it is my will and desire that all the Slaves which I hold in my own right shall receive their freedom. To emancipate them during her life, would, though earnestly wished by me, be attended with such insufferable difficulties on account of their intermixture by marriage with the dower Negroes, as to excite the most painful sensations . . . it not being in my power, under the tenure by which the dower Negroes are held, to manumit them.

And Whereas, among those who will receive freedom according to this devise, there may be some who from old age or bodily infirmities, and others who, on account of their infancy, that will be unable to support themselves, it is my will and desire that all who come under the first and second description, shall be comfortably clothed and fed by my heirs while they live; and that such of the latter description as have no parents living, or, if living, are unable or unwilling to provide for them, shall be bound by the court until they shall arrive at the age of twenty-five years. . . .

The Negroes thus bound are (by their masters or mis-

tresses) to be taught to read & write & be bro't up to some useful occupation, agreeably to the laws of the commonwealth of Virginia, providing for the support of orphan and other poor children. . . .

And I do, moreover, most pointedly and most solemnly enjoin it upon my Executors hereafter named or the survivor of them to see that this cause respecting Slaves and every part thereof, be religiously fulfilled at the epoch at which it is directed to take place, without evasion, neglect, or delay, after the crops which may then be on the ground are harvested, particularly as it respects the aged and infirm. . . .

And to my mulatto man William (calling himself William Lee) I give immediate freedom, or if he should prefer it (on account of accidents which have befallen him and which have rendered him incapable of walking or of any active employment) to remain in the situation he now is, it shall be optional in him to do so; in either case, however, I allow him an annuity of Thirty Dollars during his natural life . . . and this I give him as a testimony of my sense of his attachment to me, and for his faithful services during the Revolutionary War. . . .

The *"dower Negroes"* referred to in the excerpt were the slaves owned by Martha. She claimed them as her dower right in her first marriage to Daniel Parke Custis. President Washington had only a life interest in them by reason of his marriage to the former Mrs. Custis.

Washington's request that his freed slaves *"be taught to read & write"* was never carried out. The laws of the State of Virginia at that time expressly prohibited schools for the instruction of Negroes.

"My mulatto man William" served as Washington's attendant during the Revolutionary War until he was injured in battle and was unable to continue. William Lee grew quite famous after President Washington died and as the legend grew "William Lees" turned up everywhere. He had five different funerals—each reported as the funeral of the origi-

nal William Lee. He died once in North Carolina, once in Missouri, once in Arkansas, twice in New York.

Among the personal bequests, the following item appears:

Item: To my brother, Charles Washington, I give and bequeath the Gold headed cane left me by Dr. Franklin in his will.

The cane that passed through two famous American wills is now the property of the United States government.

★

Millions left by a New Englander to establish a home for indigent sailors of whaling ships, another estate left for the benefit of wool carders in Massachusetts, a special fund set up to ransom American seamen held by pirates on the North African coast—these are just a few of the thousands of bequests destined to become curiosity items. The causes or persons they sought to help no longer exist and the testators' good intention have been defeated by progress.

A famous case of this kind involves the estate of Bryan Mullanphy, a former mayor of St. Louis who died in 1851. In his will, Judge Mullanphy set aside $200,000

to constitute a fund to furnish relief to all poor emigrants and travelers coming to St. Louis on their way to settle the west.

As time passed it became more and more difficult to find emigrants on their way to settle the west. In 1934, living relatives of Mullanphy sought to dissolve the trust and acquire the assets, which, with interest added, was worth over a million dollars. The city of St. Louis opposed the dissolution, contending that it would be inconsistent with Judge Mullanphy's intent since he made no provision for any relatives in his will. The court found that "while the Sante Fe and the Oregon trails may be paved with concrete and poor

140

travelers may be outfitted in Model T Fords rather than Prairie Schooners, there still must be poor travelers who need assistance."

Today even the Model T has passed from the scene, but in the St. Louis railroad station and bus depot are fully staffed offices ready to help anyone who needs assistance. The sign on the door reads, "Mullanphy Traveler's Aid."

Revelations

> *Truth sits upon the lips of dying men.*
> MATTHEW ARNOLD

Some testators give away more than their property—they give themselves away. Rufus Hatch, for example. Mr. Hatch, who departed this life in 1881, advised his sons to learn a trade rather than a profession in order that "they will always be sure of an honest living." He added:

> *I earnestly desire that my children shall not gamble in any way for money, as their father has had experience sufficient for all posterity.*

★

Almost always we find consistency between a man's personality and the wishes he expresses in his will. But every once in a while there are surprises. W. C. Fields, for example. Fields made a career of hating children but his will stated that after the death of his heirs, the executor of his will should form a corporation under the name of W.C. Fields College *"for orphan white boys and girls, where no religion of any sort is to be preached. Harmony is the purpose of the thought."*

One of the beneficiaries of his will was the love of his life in his later years, Carlotta Monti. His estranged wife did not take kindly to the idea and the ensuing court squabbles and lawyer's fees left the orphanage unfunded and unrealized.

Fields, whose public hatred of children was excelled only by his private love of booze, was himself the beneficiary of a will. Claude C. Ferdinand, an old crony and juggling partner, directed in his will that W. C. Fields was to receive a case of Scotch and that Fields could select the brand.

★

Actors' Studio director Lee Strasberg was a good friend and an important influence on Marilyn Monroe. At her death Marilyn Monroe's gross estate amounted to some $90,000. After providing for her mother and friends, the rest of Marilyn's estate and all her personal effects and clothing were willed to Strasberg with instructions that he distribute them *"among my friends, colleagues and those to whom I am devoted."*

★

Novelist, wit and bonvivant Gene Fowler said that he wrote books "for his own soul's satisfaction" and not for money. In his will he said, *"The Grim Reaper has sharp elbows and is nudging me . . . I need not apologize to my heirs for the fact that I have given such small attention to the material prizes of the world. I dislike few men and can say in God's presence that I hate no man. Life has been good to me."*

★

In lieu of cash, William Hampton, who died at the beginning of this century, left his son a copy of Lawrie's

"As executor of the will —"

Drawing by Ben Roth

"Interest Tables." According to his will, this prudent Englishman did so

> . . . *not for its intrinsic value, but from the hope that so small an incident may be of use to him in future years. And I particularly recommend to him the study of the compound interest tables, as showing that from comparatively small investments, by patience, large sums may be realized.*

★

In a will written at the turn of the century, Joseph H. Melchior of Seattle disposed of $120,000 in particular and the legal profession in general:

> *I never like lawyers as a class and to keep away from them and steer clear of their inveigling schemes and grasping machination—ever an active ingredient in their diabolical profession—has been my constant life-long effort . . .*
> *The incontrovertible facts in my case are these—there never was a better, all-round individual ever set foot upon the regions of this broad state than myself.*

★

The French attorney who wrote his will at about the same time as Mr. Melchior makes a stunning reply in the never-ending dialogue between lawyer and client.

The attorney's will reads:

> *I give 100,000 francs to the local madhouse. I obtained this money out of those who pass their lives in litigation; in bequeathing it for the use of lunatics I only make restitution.*

★

John Randolph, the famous American statesman, was known throughout his life for his sharp, biting tongue. In the writing of his will, this peculiar talent did not forsake him.

As lawyers and courts of law are extremely addicted to making wills for dead men, which they never made when living, it is my will and desire that no person who shall set aside, or attempt to set aside, the will above referred to, shall ever inherit, possess, or enjoy any part of my estate. . . .

★

This is my last will,
I insist on it still;
To sneer on and welcome,
And e'en laugh your fill.
  I, William Hickington,
Poet of Pocklington,
Do give and bequeath,
As free as I breathe,
To thee, Mary Jarum
The Queen of my Harum,
My cash and my cattle,
With every chattel,
To have and to hold,
Come heat or come cold,
Sans hindrance or strife,
Though thou art not my wife.
As witness my hand,
Just here as I stand.
The twelfth of July
In the year Seventy.
        WM. HICKINGTON

William Hickington died in 1770. His rhyming will was admitted to probate at the Deanery Court in the City of York, England.

★

Excerpts from the Last Will and Testament of Philip, Fifth Earl of Pembroke:

"I, Philip, V Earl of Pembroke and Montgomery, being, as I am assured, of unsound health, but of sound memory —as I well remember that five years ago I did give my vote for the despatching of old Canterbury, neither have I forgotten that I did see my King upon the scaffold—yet as it is said that Death doth even now pursue me, and, moreover, as it is yet further said that it is my practice to yield under coercion, I do now make my last will and testament.

"Imprimis: As for my soul, I do confess I have often heard men speak of the soul, but what may be these same souls, or what their destination, God knoweth; for myself, I know not. Men have likewise talked to me of another world, which I have never visited, nor do I even know an inch of the ground that leadeth thereto. When the King was reigning, I did make my son wear a surplice, being desirous that he should become a Bishop, and for myself I did follow the religion of my master: then came the Scotch, who made me a Presbyterian, but since the time of the three principal religions of the kingdom—if any one of the three can save a soul, to that I claim to belong; if, therefore, my executors can find my soul, I desire they will return it to Him who gave it to me.

"Item: I give my body, for it is plain I cannot keep it; as you see, the chirurgeons are tearing it in pieces. Bury me, therefore; I hold lands and churches enough for that. Above all, put not my body beneath the church-porch, for I am, after all, a man of birth, and I would not that I should be interred there, where Colonel Pride was born.

"Item: I will have no monument, for then I must needs have an epitaph, and verses over my carcase: during my life I have had enough of these.

"Item: I give all my wild beasts to the Earl of Salisbury,

being very sure that he will preserve them, seeing that he refused the King a doe out of his park.

"Item: I give nothing to my Lord Saye, and I do make him this legacy willingly, because I know that he will faithfully distribute it unto the poor.

"Item: I bequeath to Thomas May, whose nose I did break at a mascarade, five shillings. My intention had been to give him more; but all who shall have seen his 'History of Parliament' will consider that even this sum is too large.

"Item: I give to the Lieutenant-General Cromwell one of my words, the which he must want, seeing that he hath never kept any of his own.

"Item: I give up the ghost."

★

Isaac Norris of Philadelphia made this poetic admonition in his will, admitted to probate in 1735:

He that perverts this will of mine
View well this lot, 'twill soon be thine.
Plain words, with obvious meaning, need no School
In wills, the Intention is the rigorous Rule.

Exit Laughing

> *Let the world slide, let the world go,*
> *A fig for care, and a fig for woe!*
> *If I can't pay, why I can owe,*
> *And death makes equal the high and low.*

The late Janis Joplin, tragic rock star of the early seventies, left $2500 to be spent on a farewell party in her honor after her death. The party was held at Lion's Share in San Anselmo, California, her favorite pub.

Wayne Morris, the movie star, died in 1959 at the age of forty-five. A portion of his will reads:

One hundred dollars shall be expended at the discretion of my closest surviving relatives for the purpose of buying booze and canapés for my friends. On second thought make it three hundred dollars because I don't want my friends to go away sober or serious.

★

Novelist Ian Fleming's will contained a clause that his fictional creation, master spy James Bond (007), might have written. Fleming left $1,400 each to three friends provided they spend the money within 19 months *"on some extravagance."* Friend number one planned to spend the money on a trip to Burma. "That will be exciting and extravagant," she said. Friend number two was going to spend his money on rare 18th century books on architecture. Friend number three hasn't collected yet: He can't decide how to spend his extravagance.

★

A case of bourbon went to J. Wesley Cupp, a Los Angeles lawyer, by the will of his friend, Edward P. Hadley, of San Diego, California, in August 1947,

he to quaff the same at his leisure, not to extend over a period longer than necessary to consume the same in the presence and company of many other of my pals in Los Angeles.

★

Jerry Hilborn has been dead for over twenty-five years but, according to the terms of his will, he has been the "host" at a dance held every year in his honor by the people of West Minot, Maine.

★

When André Fraysse found himself a widower at the tender age of twenty-three he was distraught. When he learned soon after that his wife had bequeathed a small fortune for use other than his own he was inconsolable.

On August 9, 1925, he and his mother presented themselves at the office of the local notary to argue the point. Having failed to convince the notary that the recently deceased wife was insane at the time the will was drawn, mother and son resorted to extreme methods. Mme. Fraysse snatched the will and as the notary hurled upon her to recover

156

"My goodness! Your dear old uncle seems to
have left everything to me."

Drawing by Peter Arno;
© The New Yorker Magazine, Inc.

the document she passed it quickly to her son. Then, in the words of The New York Times account of the incident, "The latter quickly put it into his mouth, chewed it violently and swallowed it without a pause, before the eyes of the astonished notary."

Unfortunately for M. Fraysse, this gastronomic feat went unrewarded. A carbon copy of the will just as effectively cut him off without a franc.

★

Edwin Orlando Swain, a tall distinguished gentleman who ran a voice culture studio in New York died in 1965 at age 82. The fact that he was penniless did not stop him from leaving a will—decorated with a red ribbon and a gold seal —which had to be one of the oddest ever filed for probate.

1. I direct that all my creditors be paid except my landlord.

2. I give and bequeath to my good friend, Theodore Weber, my best aluminum tin if I die of anything but indigestion. In that event, I give him a sad farewell.

3. To my old friend, Ann Lewis, I give and bequeath Purcell's "Passing By," which I wrongfully took and carried away last Christmas.

4. I give and bequeath to my dear friend, Mrs. George Hale, the satisfaction of being remembered in my will.

5. To my old pal, Mary Ledgerwood, I give and bequeath the sum of 35 cents. It's not much but it's the beginning of a Scotch fortune.

6. I leave to my lawyer, Huber Lewis, the task of explaining to my relatives why they didn't get a million dollars apiece.

7. I appoint Huber Lewis executor of my will. In view of his profession, I suppose we had better require him to furnish a bond. I give him full power to sell, mortgage or pledge any or all of my estate for the purpose of paying the legacy left by Article 5, and if a sufficient sum cannot be realized, I warn him to be wary of the legatee.

Swain's will was witnessed by three singers, Mme. Schumann-Heink, Louise Lurch and Marie DeKyser. Preceding their signatures was this echo from Gilbert and Sullivan's "Mikado" . . .

Three Little Maids from school are we,
Called to witness this will, you see,
And testify to its propriety
Three Little Maids from school.
Everything has been properly done,
The testator's looks suggested a "bun",
But he knew right enough we considered it fun,
Three Little Maids from school.

Swain acknowledged his poor estate and left his good humour in lieu of cash. Others are not deterred by a lack of funds and use their wills to make generous gifts without the money to back them up. Presumably its the thought that counts. Robert Ruark, the famous sportsman and novelist, left a will that reflected the size of his heart—$50,000 to his secretary, $25,000 cash to two friends, $10,000 to his housekeeper, $10,000 to his gardener—but the wherewithal to honor these gifts was sadly lacking. Ruark's publisher had to bring out two posthumous books in order to recover the money that the author owed them.

★

In a will probated in London in 1946, George Lofcoate provided £208 for the boys at the neighborhood pub to drink his health *"every Sunday at 1 p.m. as long as the money holds out."* The same year, Louis Gardiol of California passed on, leaving instructions in his will *"to set 'em up for the pallbearers"* and twelve dollars to cover the tab. Immediately after the funeral the six pallbearers complied with Gardiol's last request.

★

This lighthearted approach to a grim occasion is reminiscent of the frolic that took place in Padua on July 17, 1418. Well-documented accounts of the event tell of a joyous celebration, much more like a wedding than the funeral ceremony that it actually was. The festive atmosphere was the idea of the late Lodovico Cortusio, formerly Jurisconsultus of Padua, who spelled out carefully in his will each detail of his funeral. In accordance with the will, there was to be a feast and entertainment accompanied by *"the sound of lutes, violins, hautboys, trumpets, tambourines and other musical instruments."* Weeping by relatives or friends was absolutely forbidden and, as an incentive to merriment, an additional bequest was offered to the member of the funeral party who laughed most heartily.

★

Among the bequests of Charles A. Murray, whose will was probated in Cumberland County, New Jersey, in 1908:

I give, bequeath and devise to Lyon Post G.A.R. the sum of twenty-five dollars to buy some fun, even if they have to jump the aquarium to get it; their time is getting short so they had better get a move on.

To all my other friends and relations I leave my blessing and the assurance that I will do all I can for them up here, as soon as I find out "where I am at."

Quite different—and yet, as it turned out, not so different —was the exit of a devout Italian spinster who died in the early part of the seventeenth century.

Shocked by the irreverence of the clergy during funeral ceremonies, she took special precautions to insure the solemnity of her own leave-taking. In a special clause in her will, she declared that if any priest so much as smiled or showed any signs of levity, he was to be excluded from

"I'm afraid your uncle wasn't as wealthy as
everyone thought."

sharing in the large bequest for the benefit of the clergymen present at the ceremony.

When, at the elderly woman's death, her brother explained the unusual clause to the assembled clergymen, they expressed shock at the implication. But once the procession was under way, the priests began to eye each other with a peculiar twinkle; the ban on frivolity was a difficult one to forget. The twinkle became a smirk, the smirk a grin, the grin a smile, and finally a laugh that spread infectiously among the priests until the ceremony collapsed under gales of laughter.

The brother refused to pay any of the fees and the affair was brought before the tribunal. According to old records of the dispute, the decision was made in favor of the clergy on the ground that "the absurdity of the prohibition was in itself a provocation to violate it."

★

John B. Kelly Sr.
A Classic Will

I loved you, so I drew these tides of man unto my hands and wrote my will across the sky in stars.

Seven Pillars of Wisdom
T.E. LAWRENCE

It is ironic that an individual as colorful and unique as Jack Kelly should be generally known and referred to as "Grace Kelly's father." He was a remarkable man who never required any reflection of glory. Long before his daughter Grace became a movie star and Her Serene Highness Princess Grace of Monaco, Jack Kelly achieved eminence, rising from bricklayer to millionaire contractor. With two minor exceptions, Mr. Kelly's widow, Margaret, three daughters and a son were made the sole beneficiaries of the will.

It is difficult to say whether this colorful Irishman's unique testament will encourage and inspire others to make their own will a personal document in addition to an instrument which transfers property. It will, I think, suggest the possibilities. Jack Kelly had something to say which would not fit into the mold of legal terminology, so he said it his way without endangering the validity of the will or the rights of his heirs.

In the selected clauses that follow, Mr. Kelly speaks for himself:

For years I have been reading Last Wills and Testaments, and I have never been able to clearly understand any of them at one reading. Therefore I will attempt to write my own will in the hope that it will be understandable and legal. Kids will be called "kids" and not "issue," and it will not be cluttered up with "parties of the first part," "per stirpes," "perpetuities," "quasi-judicial," "to wit," and a lot of other terms that I am sure are only used to confuse those for whose benefit it is written.

This is my Last Will and Testament and I believe I am of sound mind. (Some lawyers will question this when they read my Will; however, I have my opinion of some of them, so that makes it even.)

Godfrey Ford has been with me over forty-five years, and has been a faithful and loyal servant. Therefore, I want him to be kept in employment as long as he behaves himself well, making due allowances for minor errors of the flesh, if being slightly on the Casanova side is an error. I want my survivors to feel an obligation regarding his comfort and employment. In addition, I give him $1,000 outright. I have already turned over to him the bonds I bought for him at Christmas each year. . . .

After providing for his daughters and son John, Kelly approaches the matter of his sons-in-law, among them Prince Rainier of Monaco:

In the case of my daughters' husbands, they do not share and if any of my daughters dies, her share goes to her children, or if there are no children, then that share goes back into my own children's fund. I don't want to give the impression that I am against sons-in-law—if they are the right type they will provide for themselves and their families

166

and what I am able to give my daughters will help pay the dress shop bills, which, if they continue as they have started out, under the able tutelage of their mother, will be quite considerable. . . .

I can think of nothing more ghastly than the heirs sitting around listening to some representative reading a Will. They always remind me of buzzards and vultures awaiting the last breath of the stricken. Therefore, I will try to spare that ordeal and let you read the Will before I go to my reward —whatever it will be. I do hope that it will never be necessary to go into Court over spoils, for to me the all-time low in family affairs is a court fight, in which I have seen families engage. If you cannot agree, I will direct that the executor or trustees, as the case may be, shall decide all questions of administration or distribution, as the executor and trustees will be of my choosing or yours. . . .

I will try to give each of you all I can during my life so that you will have money in your own right—in that way—you will not be wholly dependent on my bequest. I want you all to understand that U. S. Government Bonds are the best investment even if the return is small, and then come Commonwealths and Municipals, that have never failed to meet their interest charges. As the years gather you will meet some pretty good salesmen who will try to sell you everything from stock in a copper or gold mine to some patent that they will tell you will bring you millions, but remember, that for every dollar made that way, millions have been lost. I have been taken by this same gentry but that was perhaps because I had to learn from experience—when my father died, my hopes were high, but the exchequer low, and the stock market was on the other side of the railroad tracks, as far as I was concerned.

To Kell, I want to say that if there is anything to this Mendelian theory, you will probably like to bet on a horse or indulge in other forms of gambling—so if you do, never bet what you cannot afford to lose and if you are a loser, don't

*plunge to try to recoup. That is wherein the danger lies.
"There will be another deal, my son, and after that, another
one." Just be moderate in all things and don't deal in
excesses. (The girls can also take that advice.) I am not going
to try to regulate your lives, as nothing is quite as boring as
too many "don'ts." I am merely setting down the benefit of
my experience, which most people will admit was rather
broad, since it runs from Port Said to Hawaii, Miami Beach
to South America.*

*I have written this Will in a lighter vein because I have
always felt that Wills were so dreary that they might have
been written by the author of "Inner Sanctum" and I can see
no reason for it, particularly in my case. My family is raised
and I am leaving enough so they can face life with a better
than average start, financially.*

*As for me, just shed a respectful tear if you think I merit it,
but I am sure that you are all intelligent enough not to weep
all over the place: I have watched a few emotional acts at
graves, such as trying to jump into it, fainting, etc. but the
thoroughbred grieves in the heart. . . .*

*Not that my passing should occasion any "scenes" for the
simple reason that life owes me nothing. I have ranged far
and wide, have really run the gamut of life. I have known
great sorrow and great joy. I had more than my share of
success. Up to this writing my wife and children have not
given me any heartaches, but on the contrary, have given me
much happiness and a pardonable pride, and I want them to
know I appreciate that. I worked hard in my early life, but I
was well paid for that effort.*

*In this document I can only give you things, but if I had the
choice to give you worldly goods or character, I would give
you character. The reason I say that, is with character you
will get worldly goods because character is loyalty, honesty,
ability, sportsmanship and, I hope, a sense of humor.*

*If I don't stop soon, this will be as long as Gone With the
Wind, so just remember, when I shove off for greener*

*pastures or whatever it is on the other side of the curtain,
that I do it unafraid and, if you must know, a little curious.*

Jack Kelly dictated his will to a stenographer on April 14,
1960. He read through the typed manuscript and when he was
satisfied that everything was in order he signed it with a
flourish—in green ink.

★

> *The rest is silence.*
> HAMLET'S FINAL WORDS

ABOUT THIS VILLAGE
by Peter Douglas

"Granny Coster came into the store one day and walking up to the counter and looking me straight in the eye, said 'Cuckoo'. 'Cuckoo?' I answered.

'Cuckoo,' said Granny. I looked around at the other customers for help. A housewife spoke up. 'Cuckoo', she said. I turned to Maggie, but she shrugged and shook her head.

'Cuckoo, cuckoo', said the customers, all around the shop. The one young lady went to a shelf and taking down a tin, handed it to Granny. Granny banged the tin of cocoa down in front of me and pointed to it *'Cuckoo!'*

Here is the latest chronicle of the uproarious doings and happenings in and around a small Norfolk village—for life is never as peaceful as it ought to be for Peter Douglas and his wife Maggie at their General Store and Post Office!

S.B.N. 0 552 11671 8   Price: 95p

DOWN THE VILLAGE STREET
by Peter Douglas

An uproarious chronicle of a year's doings and happenings in a small Norfolk country village that is a riot from beginning to end. A worthy companion to the stories of James Herriot and Neil Boyd.

"It hit Maggie and I that we had really done it. For better or worse we were now heading for the rural life, the quiet village, the daydream existence. I stopped the car, and looked at Maggie. 'We've really done it,' I said. She smiled. 'I know', she said. 'You can keep all your factories and chimneys, and your motorways and smog. This is what I want to see every day.' We both looked at the quiet countryside around us. 'Yes', I agreed. 'To hell with the city'. 'Yes', said Maggie. 'And to hell with the three-legged cat'. . . ."

"It is blessed with a similar whimsical appeal (As the Herriot and Boyd books) and a strong whiff of future success. . . . brims over with joy."

Sunday Express

0 552 11256 9   95p

OH, MY DARLING DAUGHTER
by Eric Malpass

At seventeen, Viola's dreams of the future hadn't gone much further than marrying the beautiful Reverend Chisholm, the curate from St. Cuthbert's, and having ten children, so taking charge of the family while Mother was off on an eccentric jaunt was rather unexpected. Looking after an eternally grubby little brother, and a sister who knew all about sex and the Thirty Years War but little else, was no easy task—and Father didn't help when he invited the glamorous Gloria to be their 'housekeeper'. The sleepy village of Shepherd's Delight had never seen anything quite like Gloria, and neither had the beautiful Reverend Chisholm! What with that, and the mysterious postcards arriving from Mother in Cairo, Istanbul, Samarkand . . . Viola felt that life was getting out of hand . . .

0 552 10756 5   80p

LOVE IN THE DOG HOUSE
by Molly Douglas

Molly and Christopher Douglas discovered that everything could and did happen when they began to breed and board dogs on their Manitoba farm.

There were cockers, beagles, chihuahuas and Assorted others. . . . all kept in order by the Major, an elderly beagle of military bearing who kept strict discipline in the doggy ranks. There was Star, the toy terrier, who bullied the bull, and Twan Fu, the shih tzu, who arrived on a silver leash with day and night blankets, brush, comb, raincoat and choco drops, and had the time of his life rolling in cow pats and living like a real dog.

There were the people who came to buy and board, and dogs who were supposed to mate—and wouldn't. And above all there was the Douglas family, who turned their home into
THE DOG HOUSE . . .

0 552 11333 6   85p

A FATHER BEFORE CHRISTMAS
by Neil Boyd

They're back—the irrepressible Father Charles Duddleswell, the maddening, glorious Mrs. Pring and the innocent Father Neil Boyd—a series of new escapades that will have you rolling in the aisles and, for that matter, in the nave and in the vestry. Funnier and more appealing than ever. . . .

"An enchanting blend of humour and humanity." Sunday Express

0 552 11010 8   85p

THE CRACKER FACTORY
by Joyce Rebeta-Burditt

Meet Cassie Barrett . . .

Cassie is a typical suburban housewife: she has three children, a husband she isn't sure she loves, a lover she knows she doesn't, a psychiatrist she adores and wants to murder, a major drinking problem, and Cleveland's fastest, funniest mouth.

0 552 11138 4   95p

LUCIA IN LONDON
by E. F. Benson

LUCIA IN LONDON is the second hilarious novel in the famous Lucia series by E. F. Benson—a series originally published in the 1920s, when it immediately attracted a huge and distinguished cult following.

In QUEEN LUCIA, the autocratic, ostentatious and quite irrepressible Mrs. Emmeline Lucas conquered the provincial society of Riseholme. Now she has set her sights considerably higher as she prepares to lay siege to England's beau monde, glittering with duchesses and princes, prima donnas and gossip writers. Lucia, whose methods are not always beyond reproach, is guaranteed to set their tongues wagging; she gets into as many scrapes as Sir John Falstaff and makes as many gaffes as Mrs. Malaprop . . . only to escape them all, in triumph. But then, as Olga Bracely remarks, she 'could wriggle her way out of a thumb-screw' . . .

Still deliciously funny, outrageously U, quintessentially English, Benson's comic characters have come alive again for another generation.

0 552 11163 5   £1.25

SUMMER AWAKENING
by Eric Malpass

A lot could happen over the long summer holidays—and in the Pentecost household it usually did. But this summer was the most eventful yet . . . With the help of an unexpected German au pair, Gaylord was discovering that some girls came a pretty close second to boats and rugger; Momma was noticing that old friend Charles was looking at her in a strange new way, and Amanda aged ten, knew she would die if Gaylord's friend Roger married anyone else but her . . . Never did the course of love run less smoothly than in the Pentecost family but before long Gaylord was wishing the summer would never end. And Momma was fearing she'd never see the end of it.

0 552 10755 7   80p

BLESS ME FATHER
by Neil Boyd

Meet Father Neil Boyd, as he copes with his first confession, deals with a shotgun wedding, runs the parish bazaar, thwarts the local bookie, and does his best to outwit the Mother Superior of the Convent. Meet Father Charles Duddleswell, the plump, mischievous Irish parish priest who initiates Fr. Neil in the practical tricks of the priestly trade. Meet Mrs. Pring, the formidable housekeeper who alternately pampers and tyrannises her bachelor charges. Priest or Non-priest, churchgoer or atheist, Bless Me Father is a book for everyone who likes to have their ribs tickled and their sides split with helpless laughter.

0 552 10669 0   75p

A SELECTION OF FINE TITLES
IN CORGI PRINT

While every effort is made to keep prices low, it is sometimes necessary to increase prices at short notice. Corgi Books reserve the right to show new retail prices on covers which may differ from those previously advertised in the text or elsewhere.

The prices shown below were correct at the time of going to press. (Oct. '81)

☐ 10796 4	THE SECRET LEMONADE DRINKER	*Guy Bellamy*	£1.25
☐ 11163 5	LUCIA IN LONDON	*E. F. Benson*	£1.25
☐ 11187 2	MISS MAPP	*E. F. Benson*	95p
☐ 10669 0	BLESS ME, FATHER	*Neil Boyd*	75p
☐ 11010 8	A FATHER BEFORE CHRISTMAS	*Neil Boyd*	85p
☐ 11149 X	IMOGEN	*Jilly Cooper*	£1.00
☐ 10878 2	PRUDENCE	*Jilly Cooper*	£1.00
☐ 10576 7	HARRIET	*Jilly Cooper*	£1.00
☐ 10818 9	THE CEDAR TREE: A BOUGH BREAKS	*Michael Hardwick*	80p
☐ 10438 8	THE CEDAR TREE: AUTUMN OF AN AGE	*Michael Hardwick*	75p
☐ 10755 7	SUMMER AWAKENING	*Eric Malpass*	80p
☐ 10756 5	OH, MY DARLING DAUGHTER	*Eric Malpass*	80p
☐ 10626 7	THE LONG, LONG DANCES	*Eric Malpass*	75p
☐ 10625 9	MORNING'S AT SEVEN	*Eric Malpass*	70p
☐ 98081 1	THE FRANK MUIR BOOK	*Frank Muir*	£1.95
☐ 09891 4	CHIA THE WILDCAT	*Joyce Stranger*	70p
☐ 09462 5	LAKELAND VET	*Joyce Stranger*	70p

CORGI BOOKS, Cash Sales Department, P.O. Box 11 Falmouth, Cornwall. Please send cheque or postal order, no currency.

U.K. Please allow 40p for the first book, 18p for the second book and 13p for each additional book ordered, to a maximum charge of £1.49

B.F.P.O. & EIRE please allow 40p for the first book; 18p for the second book plus 13p per copy for the next three books, thereafter 7p per book.

Overseas customers. Please allow 60p for the first book plus 18p per copy for each additional book.

NAME (block letters) ....

ADDRESS ....

(Oct. '81) ....